John Vizard

Narrative of a Tour Through France, Italy, and Switzerland

In a series of letters

John Vizard

Narrative of a Tour Through France, Italy, and Switzerland
In a series of letters

ISBN/EAN: 9783744755665

Printed in Europe, USA, Canada, Australia, Japan

Cover: Foto ©Andreas Hilbeck / pixelio.de

More available books at **www.hansebooks.com**

NARRATIVE

OF A

TOUR

THROUGH

FRANCE, ITALY,

AND

SWITZERLAND,

IN A

SERIES OF LETTERS.

LONDON:
SIMPKIN AND MARSHALL, STATIONERS' HALL COURT.
DURSLEY:
JAMES WHITMORE, STAMP OFFICE, LONG STREET.
1872.

PREFACE.

—oo—

THESE Letters were written in the year 1867 during a Continental tour, undertaken by the advice of my physicians, in order to obtain for a time that entire relief from business which was considered indispensable for me. They were addressed to my Family at home, without the slightest notion that they would ever appear in print, nor had such a thought occurred to me since, until a recent circumstance suggested it to my mind. I then showed the MS. to my Bookseller, who at once offered to publish it at his own pecuniary risk.

Since the Letters were written, the Papal territory has become annexed to the present Kingdom of Italy, and the solemnities of Holy Week and Easter at Rome, as hereinafter described, have consequently ceased and may never again be witnessed. This circumstance may communicate some special interest to that portion of the narrative, while the fact of the tour being my first visit to the Continent (except for a single day in Belgium on business, many years ago) will impart to the whole the strength and freshness of first impressions. I was accompanied by my younger son A—— until we reached Paris on my route homewards, and by my niece E—— afterwards, and they are referred to in the Letters by those initials. The reader will not be surprised to hear, considering the toil and excitement attending the events of my journey, that the object for which it was taken, as regards the recovery of my health, failed ultimately of effect. Nevertheless, the retrospect will always be a source of enjoyment to me, and I can truly say in the words of Virgil:

Hæc olim meminisse juvabit, (a)

while inviting my reader to join me in the next line:

Per varios casus, per tot discrimina rerum,
Tendimus in Latium.

J. V.

Ferney Hill, Dursley.
Oct., 1872.

(a) Æneid. lib. 1

CONTENTS.

	PAGE.
Paris	1
Lyons	14
Marseilles	16
Genoa	19
Leghorn	25
Pisa	26
Florence	28, 31
Rome	33, 87
Naples and Vesuvius	69
Herculaneum and Pompeii	74
Sorrento	75
Bale	84
Ancona	89, 91
Ravenna	90
Bologna	92
Venice	95
Milan	99
Monza	102
The Italian Lakes	104
S. Gothard Pass	107
Lucerne	111
Interlaken	114
The Mürren	115
Berne	117
Frohburg, Strasbourg, and Basle	120
Zurich	121
Chamounix	122
Appendix	129

Narrative &c.

—oo—

Paris, March 9th, 1867.

We left Charing Cross Station at 9.54 a.m. for Paris, and, except for about two hours and a half in crossing from Folkestone to Boulogne, had an agreeable journey. The first thing that strikes you on arriving in France is the reverse occupation of the sexes, compared with what it is in England; for a number of women enter the steamboat from the shore to unlade her of the passengers' luggage, whereas at the hotels men do the office of chambermaid; the women also were working in the fields between Boulogne and Paris. This part of the country is flat and uninteresting, and much of it under water. There was a wonderful wooden bridge across an arm of the sea, having thirty-six arches. The soil is chalk, with about six inches of mould. Amiens, where we stopped for refreshment, is a fine-looking town; here, I believe, the Treaty of Peace with Bounaparte was signed in 1802.

We arrived in Paris about 9.0 p.m., and had to endure the farce of having our luggage searched, as they call it, at the Custom House, but which is little more than the trouble of unpacking and repacking it again. After some delay, in consequence of a wrong direction, we got to our boarding-house, Madame Taylor's, 94, Champs Elysées, at about ten o'clock. There are forty boarders in the house, all English or American. Sunday was a very wet and cold day. We sallied forth, after breakfast, to the new Russo-Greek church, built by subscriptions from Russia at an expense of £48,000. The church is exceedingly handsome; the worshippers were partly Russians and partly Greeks: they could be distinguished by their faces. The space is quite open and carpeted, but females are accommodated with chairs, as they come in. It was a mass, and four priests officiated in handsome-coloured vestments. During the service the worshippers seemed to stand, sit, or kneel *ad libitum*, but they were continually crossing themselves; and when they knelt, showed great signs of devotion, bowing down occasionally with their faces to the ground. There was an interesting ceremony of two infant communions—a mother bringing up her child to the priest on the steps of the sanctuary, when the sacrament was brought forth from within the screen with great ceremony, the people all falling down, and the priest administering it to the little child; but there was no other administration that day. All the service was chanted, sometimes antiphonally by the priest and choir, and sometimes by the choir alone. The latter was entirely vocal, and the singing, both for the voices and the time, splendid. The service closed by the chief priest bringing out a gilded crucifix, when some service was held in connection with it, and then all the worshippers came up and kissed it, one by one, as he presented it to them. The church was filled with beautiful paintings of events in scripture history, chiefly from the New Testament, and was highly ornamented, but no images. Upon the whole, I was much pleased with what I witnessed of this Greek service; for although I understood not a word that was said, there seemed much reality about it, and the devotion of the worshippers very earnest.

At three in the afternoon we went to Notre Dame cathedral, and arrived in the middle of a sermon, by Père Felix, a famous Lent preacher. The nave was nearly filled; almost all were men, and the preacher was extremely earnest and fluent: beyond which I can answer for nothing. Immediately it was over, the great congregation from the nave left, and a new service began in the choir, which was chanted throughout, and attended by many priests and other assistants. The west front of Notre Dame is very handsome, much more so than the exterior of Westminster Abbey; but the interior falls in as great a degree below it. In the evening we went, at 7.30, to Mr. Archer Gurney's church, which is nothing more than a large room fitted up. He and an American clergyman performed the service; and the latter preached a charity sermon, full of the details of the new Italian Reformation; after which a collection was made for the poor priests, who were being starved instead of burnt to death, for conscience sake.

On Monday morning we walked through the gardens of the Tuileries to the Hôtel de Louvre, and passed through the Place de la Concorde, the most magnificent part of Paris, and in a few weeks hence, when the trees are out in leaf, I can imagine it unsurpassed by any city in the world. The climate and atmosphere are as fine and clear as on the Cotswold Hills, giving the place all the charms of the country, with the stir and splendour of the town. After visiting the Palais Royal, we went to the Tomb of Napoleon, which altogether baffles description. His remains lie in an immense marble sarcophagus under a splendid dome, before a magnificent altar constructed after the pattern of the High Altar at St. Peter's at Rome. There are four sidechapels around it, in one of which (a very handsome one) lie entombed the remains of Jerome

Buonaparte, and in another those of Joseph Buonaparte. After feasting our sight with this most interesting and magnificent place, we engaged a guide, who conducted us over the Hôtel des Invalides, where 200 old French soldiers are provided for, some of the Old Empire wearing the medal of St. Helena. We saw, also, the Chapel des Invalides, in which are suspended flags taken in Napoleon's victories: and among others we saw two flags of England. We next drove to Ste. Chapelle—a most splendid specimen of mediæval Gothic—far surpassing anything I have seen in England. It was built by St. Louis, to hold the relics which he brought from the Holy Land in the Crusade. The chapel was broken into at the first revolution, and most of the relics thrown into the Seine; but some few were preserved, and are to be seen at Notre Dame. We next visited the Palais de Justice (or Law Courts), but as it was late, the courts had done sitting. Then we went to the Morgue, where are deposited for public recognition the bodies of those who are found dead, and are not known; happily there were none there to-day. Afterwards we went to the Temple of the Pantheon, being a church in honour of the great men of France. Underneath it are the catacombs, and over them vaults containing the remains of these great men. There we saw the tombs of Voltaire and

Rousseau, and a full-length statue of the former; thence to the church of St. Geneviéve, the patron Saint of Paris, containing a brass shrine to her, near which were placed the crutches of those who believed they had been miraculously cured by her intercession. The chapel contains a most beautiful carved stone screen.

March 13th.—Yesterday we spent the greater part of our time at the Louvre, of which everyone has heard so much, that it is needless to describe. It has the largest, if not the finest, collection of paintings in Europe; a large museum of sculpture; many curiosities connected with the Kings of France; and one room devoted to things connected with the first Napoleon. We have our Guide every day, who knows all about everything, and is a great help and advantage to us. The remainder of our time we gave to the Hôtel de Cluny—full of antiquarian national curiosities. To-day we have done a good deal, having visited the church of St. Eustache, which is very fine, and far exceeds Notre Dame. We afterwards saw the Central Markets, erected by Napoleon III. At the fish stalls they contrive to have running water conveyed, and live fish kept in it—so that you may be sure of having it fresh. We then visited St. Roch church, and thence to the Gobelin Tapestry and Carpet Manufactory, which surpasses all I have seen. The colours and execution of the carpeting produce an effect superior to the best painting in the Louvre—it is the very highest perfection of art. There was a full-length likeness of the Empress, of exquisite beauty. Lastly, we visited the Treasures at Notre Dame: but I will not attempt a description of them—so splendid, and full of interest;—curiosities, chiefly donations of Kings and Emperors on great occasions. Among other things were the robes worn by Pius VII., when he crowned Napoleon; the coronation robes of the latter; a *monstrance* of surpassing brilliancy given by Louis XVIII., on the baptism of the Duke de Bourdeaux, all the coruscations being diamonds and the whole most magnificent. I must not omit to mention, among other curiosities, our day's luncheon, that is, of the three including the guide, at a restaurant. The first course was twelve snails in their shells. A—— looked very shy at the new dish; but I at last made a desperate thrust at one with my fork, and pulled him out quite black, and popped him into my mouth. A—— followed, but we did not finish the dish. I forgot to say, that, before that, we had oysters. After the snails came a mutton chop and beef steak; and our last course was fricasseed frogs, which are really quite a delicacy. These we eat without much scruple. I do not dislike French cookery.

14th.—We have to-day visited the Corps Législatif (French House of Commons). The interior is very fine and beats our Lower House, we think. There is a magnificent bust of the present Emperor there, cut out of one block of marble. From thence we went to Notre Dame de Lorette, a very beautiful church; then lunched, but not off snails this time: afterwards we visited the Emperor's stables, which are well worth seeing, and are got up in a most costly style,—marble mangers, &c. He has 360 horses, and nearly the same number of carriages, some of them, including the state carriages, are at Versailles; we saw his state saddle and bridle, and also the saddle he used at Solfarino. Thence we went to the Hôtel de Ville (the Guildhall of Paris); most splendid apartmants, and a magnificent ball room, where in 1853 a ball was given to Queen Victoria. We then went to the Luxembourg (the French House of Lords). The Throne-room is the most magnificent room in Paris, and the paintings on the walls of one of the rooms, called Marie de Medicis, by *Rubens*, *Vandyke*, *Paulo Veronese*, &c., are so valuable that it is impossible to put an estimate upon them. After this we called on Mr. H——, a Gloucestershire man, who came over here when quite young as an assistant in a woollen warehouse, and has become the head of the establishment, which, he says, is the largest in the world. He has manufactories in many parts of France. We went over his establishment, and are to dine with him to-morrow evening. This finished our day, and we drove to Madame Taylor's, along the Boulevards. It is out of the way being in the Champs Elysées, but her charges are moderate. We pay £1 a day for the two.

16th March.—Yesterday morning we went to the Louvre, and spent some time in looking over the Assyrian, Grecian, &c. courts. There are some curiosities brought from Jerusalem, and, among others, an ornamented stone sarcophagus, said to be that of King David. We did not however stay long, being anxious to get to Notre Dame to hear the famous preacher Père Hyacinthe, and witness the exposition of the sacred reliques, which are shown to the faithful every Friday in Lent. We had to be there an hour and a half before service began at 2 p.m., to get seats. The whole cathedral was filled with respectably-dressed persons, almost without exception in black (it being Lent). During the long time we waited before the sermon began, the vast congregation behaved with great quietness and reverence, and there was none of that conversation going on, which is so offensive in Westminster Abbey during the brief interval before service there—indeed, most of the persons present had their books of devotion and employed themselves with them. It is all very fine for us English to talk of the irreligion and infidelity of the French, but I should like to know whether in our metropolis, with its three millions and a half, there could be found anything like the congregation on a week-day in either of its cathedral churches to hear the finest preacher, as appeared yesterday in the cathedral of Paris, with its one million and a half. In reverence and decorum they very far surpass us, except in one particular, which is a foreign habit and seems to be thought nothing of, namely, the odious one of hawking and spitting. Even two priests that were sitting with the congregration near us did it. Another thing was rather odd: having my little opera glass, and not being able to see very well, I took it out and had a good stare at Père Hyacinthe through it, being half afraid all the time what the congregation would think of me, but I was relieved of all alarm by one of the two priests borrowing it and having a good look through it himself. In short, in these and many other things, the French are quite opposite to us, and *vice versâ*. The sermon was nearly an hour and a half long, the preacher extremely fluent and earnest, and the congregation hanging on his lips, but of course I could not unfortunately understand a word of it. That, however, which I really went for followed. You must know that that exquisite building which I mentioned before, the Sainte Chapelle, was so called, because it was built to hold the relics which St. Louis*(a)* brought from the Holy Land, having bought them of Baldwin the Emperor there for two millions of francs, in the 13th century. There were the thorns from our Lord's crown and one of the nails of the true cross. St. Louis carried them barefoot through the streets to Sainte Chapelle, where they were deposited. The chapel was broken into at the first revolution and the relics removed to Notre Dame. After the sermon yesterday these sacred relics in their reliquaries, that is, glass cases in gold frames, were produced from the altar, and a great part of the congregation went up and knelt in rows at the altar rails. The priests brought them round and each kissed them and then rose and went away, just in the same manner as in the administration of the Holy Communion in the Church of England. A—— and I went and knelt down with the rest and kissed the reliquaries. Their contents were quite visible through the glass, though it was only the case that was kissed. There were three, one containing the thorns, another one of the nails, and another part of the wood of the true cross.

(a) Louis IX. King of France.

In my former letter I mentioned having heard the celebrated preacher Père Felix last Sunday. I have since heard that last Lent he reclaimed 6,000 infidels by his preaching, and that he preaches especially to *men*, which accounts for there being no women in the nave of the cathedral last Sunday. I forgot to say in my last that when we were at the Madeline we witnessed a Roman Catholic marriage, and at St. Roch a funeral service. It was quite late when we came out of Notre Dame, and after having some refreshment at a café we got home in time to prepare for Mr. H——'s entertainment, to which we had been invited. This was at the principal restaurant in Paris. The company were chiefly gentlemen, and we were twenty-one in number—partly English and partly French. It is impossible to describe the specimen we there had of French luxuries. Course after course followed of the choicest and most delicate dishes, and the wines were perfection—indeed, I may say, I never really tasted champagne before. Mr. H—— gives one of these every week. Among the other dainties were frogs, which are really very good picking. The art of luxury, like every other in Paris, seems brought to its highest perfection;—it is not so much the quantity as the number and variety of the dishes and viands — their exquisite taste and the splendid style.

To-day,—after leaving my doctor, we spent the remainder of the day at the Louvre, examining the statuary and paintings. A most interesting room is the *Salle des Rois*, containing a number of curiosities belonging to the Kings of France from Childeric to the present time; among others, the Book of Hours, sword, sceptre, &c., of Charlemagne; the Breviary of St. Louis, and the bronze font in which he was baptized, and many most interesting *souvenirs* of the unfortunate Bourbons. But there is one whole room devoted to curiosities belonging to Napoleon I., as much space being given to him as to all the other monarchs of France together. By the way, we saw the Emperor returning from his drive in the Champs Elysées to-day, but not near enough to have a distinct view of him. We had applied for tickets of admission at the Chapel of the Tuileries to-morrow, but they have not come, so I suppose we shall miss seeing him, the Empress, and Prince Imperial.

Sunday. — Went to St. Eustache — High Mass—this morning; music and singing the best in Paris. Afterwards to the Synagogue to see two Jewish marriages; — one of the brides being daughter of the chief Rabbi. The place was crowded with men and women, and to see myself surrounded by these children of Abraham, with Hebrew texts and the names of all the Old Testament Saints painted round the walls, gave one an intense feeling of interest. One of the bridesmaids went round collecting. On Tuesday, after paying a farewell visit to Dr. T——, who has greatly improved my hearing, and strengthened my sight, we finished with a delightful drive in an open voiture round the Bois de Boulogne, a most beautiful park, and which, with the Champs Elysées and the Place de la Concorde, is the most fashionable part of Paris,— the whole forming, indeed, a terrestrial elysium.

Marseilles, 23rd March. — On Wednesday morning, with an unwilling heart, I left Paris, for I was really charmed with the place, and we were exceedingly comfortable in our *Pension*, where we met very agreeable company. You ask how we spent the evenings. After dinner, which was at six, we adjourned to the drawing-room, where the evening passed in reading, or agreeable conversation, intermixed occasionally with the game of "post," in an adjoining room. On Tuesday evening they got up some dancing. In fact, I tore myself away from Paris, which we left at 10 a.m. on Wednesday for the express train to Lyons, in order to break the journey. The country was very uninteresting, and we arrived there about 10 p.m. I had a bad night at the Grand Hôtel, for the journey was too much for me. We sallied forth the next morning with a *commissionaire* to visit the workshops of the silk manufactures, and saw the weaving. I could hardly drag myself along until after luncheon, which refreshed me, and we got into a voiture and visited the cathedral, and some of the churches, also the Palais de Justice, where we heard a cause being tried. We wound up with a visit to the Fourvier Hill, where there is a view said to exceed any in Italy or Switzerland; but the atmosphere was so thick we could not see much of it; that, however, was magnificent; had it been clear we should have seen the Alps and Mont Blanc. Among other places we visited the church of St. Irénée (as the French call him), bishop of Lyons, the disciple of Polycarp, who was disciple of St. John, and went to his tomb in the crypt, where also is set apart a place for the bones of the martyrs who suffered at Lyons under the persecution of the Emperor Severus. By the way, I forgot to mention the museum, where we saw some splendid Roman remains found in the city. Lyons is a great place for convents, &c. It is a very fine city, and the second largest in France. In the evening we went to buy a revolver in preparation for our journey to Italy, everything being so very dear in Paris. We had a capital dinner at the Table d'Hôte. I reckoned the courses, which were ten, besides dessert, and the charge was only four francs, or three shillings and sixpence each. Next night I slept off my fatigue, and started at 10 a.m. yesterday, by a second class train for Marseilles, and arrived here about eleven. This long journey again knocked me up and gave me a bad night, and I am now sitting in my bedroom writing this letter, instead of going out;—these long railway journeys beat me and throw me back, so I have determined to go from hence by water, however unpleasant. A great part of the country, yesterday, was like that from Paris to Lyons, cultivated with the vine and wheat; indeed I have only seen one cow and a few sheep all the way from Boulogne to Marseilles, and scarcely any farm buildings; but before we came to Avignon, the country wore a very different aspect, and looked like a vast garden covered with olive and mulberry trees, and apple, pear, and other fruit trees in full blossom, interspersed with many houses, where the silk worms are bred. This was bounded by the range of the Alps at no great distance, and presented a very fine scenery. The heat here is very great. We are in the Grand Hôtel. The churches in Paris and Lyons are always open, and at whatever hour we go in we find persons at their private devotions in them. The cathedral at Lyons is finer than Notre Dame. At the *buffet*, yesterday, at Avignon, Madame gave me as a stranger a beautiful nosegay, which I keep in my room. I am charmed with French politeness: not a word is said without "*si'l vous plait*," and everyone seems in good humour. I blunder out conversation with them, and they never laugh, but assist me very politely. A—— gets on capitally in conversation with them.

Marseilles, March 26th.—As I strolled along the streets yesterday and Sunday, I dropt into every church, and observed all that was going on; for yesterday, being the Feast of the Annunciation, was a great day with the people here. I have not time to tell you all I have witnessed and pondered over, but a person must come abroad and judge for himself, before he can form any sound opinion of the practical state of Romanism. All we read is partial, or contradictory. I have already visited numerous churches at various services, and at their private devotions, and have formed a pretty decided opinion; but I reserve it for the present, till I have seen Italy. The churches are open all day long, mass beginning at 4.0 a.m., and continuing till twelve; and after that, people are to be seen at all hours at their private devotions. On Sunday morning we went to the English chapel, where service was read by the British Consul—the chaplain, Mr. Douglas, being too ill to attend. There was a pretty good sprinkling of people. The day before we dropt in at the Jews' synagogue (their Sabbath) during the afternoon service. On Sunday afternoon we attended the vesper service at the church of Notre Dame de la Garde, where all persons go to make their offerings who have escaped dangers, particularly at sea, and where sailors go to ask protection before going to sea. It is situated on an eminence commanding a magnificent view of the town and sea, surrounded by mountains—a perfect panorama. It was rebuilt last year, and its consecration was attended by 44 cardinals, archbishops, and bishops, with a procession two miles long. The entire walls of the church are covered with pictures in frames, as offerings to the Virgin, describing the particular dangers, for deliverance from which they have been offered, and including every possible accident or calamity you can conceive. Here is a child falling over the banister of the stairs; another thrown off a runaway horse; another upset in a carriage; most of them persons sick in bed, with a consultation of doctors; but in each of them is represented the Virgin as bestowing the aid: there were also many models of ships given by seamen for deliverances. It is altogether the most curious collection imaginable. Some of the inscriptions I have copied out; but the most striking feature in the whole, is a full length image of the Virgin in solid silver, adorned with a crown, robes, and embroidery, over the high altar, to which all these wonderful deliverances are attributed. There were so many masses there yesterday (at some of which I was present) that A—— says, he saw about forty priests coming away in the afternoon, to say nothing of all the masses going on in all the other churches. The city is large and fine, and the hotel here always teeming with people going by or coming from the steamers. This morning it was full of people arrived from Bombay. I have fallen in with a pleasant gentlemanly Parsee on his way to Paris, whom I hope to meet again there. We have taken our places in a French steamer for Naples, which starts at nine to-morrow morning. The heat is very great here.

Genoa, 30th March.—We landed here at 8.0 a.m. on Thursday, the 28th, after a very rough voyage from Marseilles. There was a great swell in the sea, and the vessel rolled from side to side like a huge cradle. A—— was taken ill first. I was dreadfully ill. A gentleman kindly gave me some chlorodyne, which relieved me for the time, but I became so ill again, that but for a dose of chlorodyne I do not think I could have survived it. Consequently we did not proceed in the evening for Naples in the same steam packet, but arranged with the captain to wait for the next, which leaves this on Monday evening. I am glad we did not go on Thursday evening, for a violent storm of thunder and lightning and rain came on at night, and two merchant vessels were wrecked against the breakwater here close to shore, on the same day, one at four in the afternoon, and the other at ten at night—an event which had not happened for ten years before, so that, if I had gone that night, it would probably have been the death of me. Yesterday we went to the cathedral, and saw some of the churches, and the finest private picture galleries at the Palazzo Brignole Sala, and the Palazzo Balbi;—that is, some we visited Thursday, some yesterday; also beautiful private gardens, where the camellias, azaleas, &c., were out in full blossom, and numerous orange and lemon trees with their fruit hanging on them. As to paintings, I may say I never saw any before worthy the name, compared with the Italian School; they are the most magnificent feast to the eye imaginable. This city is called "The City of Palaces," as some of the streets consist only of the palaces of the old aristocracy, where are magnificent picture galleries, which they kindly allow to be seen by the public, with a permit. The view of the city from the sea is very beautiful, as it lies on the side of a hill like Bath or Clifton. Of churches, the most beautiful I have seen is that of L'Annunciata here, and I cannot imagine that even St. Peter's at Rome can surpass it in kind, though, of course, it would in degree. The church bells wake one up before 6.0 a.m., and services are going on till late in the evening. I stray into every one I can find, and there are between 90 and 100 here. The head-dress of the women of the higher and middle classes is very becoming, consisting of a muslin scarf pinned to the hair, and falling over the arms and shoulders: the lower orders wear a long printed calico scarf of gaudy colours.

The guides here do not speak English, and we do not get on so well with them as at Paris. Yesterday we visited a very interesting place— one of the *Conservatorie* here, being a kind of convent for female orphans, founded by *Fieschi*. It contains 250 inmates, who are employed upon lace and embroidery, but especially in making artificial flowers, their time being divided between this kind of work and devotion. We were shown all over it, and purchased some of the flowers. I am not sorry we were detained here, as there is much to see. Since writing the above, we have been to see two more splendid Palazzos, one the Palazzo Durazzo, the most magnificent mansion I ever saw, but chiefly for its splendid furniture and decorations. It belongs to a marquis, but surpasses anything regal I have ever seen. The apartments contain first-rate paintings. We afterwards visited the Palazzo Reale, or Royal Palace, which is not so fine as the other. The marble staircase and the colonnade give a very handsome effect to the exterior. The city is said to rank for beauty next after Naples and Constantinople. We fell in with many Americans, some sensible and intelligent, others odious and disgusting from their conceit, arrogance, and vulgarity. We are at a very comfortable hotel, kept by an Englishwoman.

April 1st.—Yesterday we attended morning and afternoon service at the English chapel, the whole arrangement being anything but satisfactory. I dropped into several Roman Catholic churches, that of the Annunciata in the evening. The service was very striking; it seemed like a broken relic of the old temple service at Jerusalem—three priests kneeling before the altar, and the congregation kneeling on the bare floor behind them, chanting the service together with the pealing organ, while clouds of incense rose up from the censers in the priests' hands. I also attended a fine vesper service on Saturday evening at St. Syr, where a priest chanted antiphonally with the organ and people, and with a splendid voice. The Italian words roll forth magnificently in chanting. To-day there was a large morning congregation at St. Syr, and a sermon, which gave me an excellent opportunity of hearing what good Italian was like. Although there is much, indeed almost everything, in continental Religion, that has the advantage of ours as regards external worship and, apparently, internal devotion, yet there is a painful fact, which casts a blight on it all, I mean the unquestionable worship of images. The sides of every church are made up of small chapels dedicated to some saint, and whose image or picture, generally the former, is set up there. You never go into a church without seeing persons praying and directing their eyes to the image in these chapels. I know the answer is, "that is the vulgar error of the common people, for which the church is not responsible;" but what are the poor people to believe, when I heard a priest, preaching at Marseilles, in the middle of his sermon from the altar-steps, turn round and make a passionate appeal to the large silver image of the Virgin on the high altar, and entreat her to look down on her *petits enfans?* Besides, the churches are more or less adorned with offerings made to saints, chiefly the Blessed Virgin, for deliverances and cures. I saw a number of pictures representing answers to prayer around the image of St. Joseph, with the words at the bottom: "*Ite Joseph.*" Among the great paintings, for one of the Ascension of our Lord, you will see fifty of the Assumption of the Virgin. But what has struck me most in Italy is, that on the chasuble worn by the priests in celebrating mass is not the Cross, as seen in Roman Catholic chapels in England, but the monogram of the Virgin thus, M, the middle part of the M being a V. A re-union, or peace with Rome, as she is, I feel is utterly impossible, and the Society for promoting the Union of Christendom to be in pursuit of a mere dream. I can think and say nothing of it but "*Delenda est!*" "O daughter of Babylon, who art to be destroyed!" I say not this in any spirit of English prejudice or self-complacency, for the Church of England is not in a condition to throw any stones at Rome, but from slow and painful conviction. There is, of course, a great residuum of sound Christian faith and practice left, which has been handed down from the Apostolic age, but the additions and incrustations cast upon it make the whole system appear one of frightful image-worship. Confessions are continually going on in the churches, but I have never seen one *man* at confession. Indeed, I have been told and believe, that the great mass of the Italians are lapsing into infidelity. In fact, I am shocked and horrified at the state of modern Christendom, and look rather to the poor Jew, whom we saw in the synagogue at Marseilles go up and touch the fold of the covering of the Law, and then kiss his hand which had so touched it. His time must and will, I believe, soon come, for that of the Gentiles, who have so abused their privileges, cannot last much longer. My pen has been running on with my thoughts; the idea of such Christianity as is witnessed abroad must be repulsive and odious to the despised children of Abraham.

Florence, April 4th.—I presume my two letters from Genoa have been received. On Monday night, about nine o'clock, we embarked on board that horrible steamer, and although the weather was quite calm and the sea smooth, and notwithstanding the chlorodyne, I had a most miserable night, no sleep—and was obliged to leave my berth in the middle of the night and lie on deck, shivering with the cold, till we reached Leghorn, between seven and eight o'clock, and was ill there also. I therefore made a firm resolve, although we had paid our fare to Naples, nothing should induce me to get into one of those detestable things again. A—— slept well, and I was the only person on board that was ill. A sad event took place on board, about three o'clock a.m. A seaman who was in the steamer died suddenly, supposed to be from an affection of the heart. This created some delay in our landing, which was not allowed to take place until after an examination by the authorities, a doctor being sent to investigate the cause of the death. When we landed at Leghorn in a small boat, there was a strange sight, a number of men attired in black robes, with black masks over their faces reaching to their breasts, and holes for their eyes; having a bier, a lighted lamp on a pole, and a cross. These, on enquiry, I found to be a party going to our vessel to bring the corpse on shore. They belonged to a fraternity called the *Societá della Misericordia*, which is established in Italy, and is composed of gentlemen only, and their object is to attend the poor in sickness, get them conveyed to hospitals, and when dead to bury them. Where shall we look in England for such an institution as this! Within an hour's time after this death was heard of in Leghorn, this party of laymen were on their way to the vessel to take charge of the body of a poor Calabrian sailor. As there was nothing to see at Leghorn, we took the first train to Pisa about 2.30, and arrived there in time to visit the Cathedral and Leaning Tower and *Campo Santo* that day, besides the workshops of a famous sculptor. I will not attempt to describe the three former places, as you may read an account of them in any description of Italy. The façade of the cathedral is the most beautiful piece of architecture I have ever seen, at least till I came here, for beauties of art so crowd on one, that one scarcely knows which to praise most. But I must not forget Nature. The approach to Leghorn from the sea was very striking; on one side was the Isle of Elba, and on the other a splendid range of the snow-capped Maritime Alps, which, with the early sun upon them, looked most picturesque. In the cathedral of Pisa was a famous lamp, the oscillation of which is said to have first suggested to Galileo the theory of the pendulum. The Campanile or Leaning Tower you of course have heard of; it is a very curious and beautiful piece of architecture; but the most interesting of these sights was the *Campo Santo*, a most exquisite building, erected to surround the earth, brought by an archbishop from Mount Calvary in the 12th century in fifty-three vessels. The holy soil is still there, and the building which encloses it is filled with antiquities and works of art. But I have forgotten the Baptistry, another most beautiful building. I bought stereoscopic views of them all. "Murray" says, these four buildings, the Cathedral, Baptistry, Campanile, and Campo Santo "are as interesting a group of buildings as any four edifices in the world." The statuary which we saw in a workman's shop of elaborate marble, dug from the neighbourhood, was beautiful beyond description,—no place like Italy for the arts! We slept at Pisa, which is a very pretty place, and glad I was to get a night's rest. The next morning we visited the church of *Santa Maria della Spina*, on the bank of the Arno, an architectural gem, and which derives its name from a thorn of our Saviour's crown, brought from the Holy Land by a merchant of Pisa, and presented to it by his descendants. It was market-day, which gave me an opportunity of seeing the country people. The cattle were splendid, but horses poor and small. We left Pisa at middle-day, and had a pleasant ride of three hours by train to Florence. The country throughout was one great garden, cultivated with vines trained up the trees, particularly the elm, and as we approached the city, the snow-capped Apennines added much to the effect of the scenery, which all around was very beautiful; indeed, as you know, Florence is famous for the loveliness of its situation. We took a guide at 4.0 p.m., and had two hours sight-seeing before dinner. The places we visited were the cathedral, which with its tower is a most magnificent piece of architecture, and the Cupola served as a model to Michael Angelo for that of St. Peter's at Rome. The Bell-Tower was designed by Giotto, and begun by him A.D. 1334, in consequence of a dream, commanding him to construct an edifice, which in height and richness of workmanship should surpass any structure raised by the Greeks or Romans in the most palmy days of their power. You may conceive, therefore, what it must be. In connection with the cathedral is the splendid baptistry, a separate building, as it is at Pisa. Then we went to the church of *La Santissima Annunziata*, a most gorgeous and splendid building, dedicated to the Virgin. In one of the inside chapels immense wealth has been lavished in honour of a miraculous fresco of the Annunciation, painted by Angels, according to popular belief; it is covered with a curtain and exposed only on extraordinary occasions. Our guide told us it was adorned with precious stones, and as much as £8000 sterling has lately been expended on a new crown for the Virgin in this miraculous picture. Next, we visited the church of *Santa Croce*, the principal church in Florence, where the remains of Michael Angelo and of Galileo lie, and to whom handsome monuments are erected, as well as to Dante, Alfiere, Machiavelli, and others. There is also a handsome full-length statue of Dante in one of the piazzas here.

Thursday.—We have had a great treat to-day. First, we visited the church of *San Luago*, and then the Laurentian Library, which consists of 10,000 MSS. given by one of the Medicis. Here I had a feast for the eyes, indeed; the original Decree of the Council of Florence, with the autographs to it of Pope Eugenius and the other Western Bishops, Anthony Patriarch of Constantinople, and the Eastern Bishops, and of the Emperor Palæologus; also old MSS. of Sophocles, Æschylus, and Homer, the earliest MS. of Virgil, autographs of Petrarch, &c. Next, we visited the house where Michael Angelo was born and died, and which is filled with souvenirs of him, original designs, &c. I sat in his little studio, had his slippers in my hand, saw his sword, stick, &c., and two of his autograph letters, and was in the room in which he died. Then we went to see a famous picture of the Lord's Supper, said to be equal to that of Leonardo de Vinci, and in better preservation. This is by *del Sarto*. Afterwards, we went over the Palazzo Pitti Picture Gallery, one of the best in Florence; the pictures few, but all first rate, including the original of Raphael's celebrated Madonna; then to the Boboli gardens, from the top of which is a splendid view of the city and surrounding country, all studded with villas most picturesque, and backed by the Apennines. Then we took a drive round the Cascine, three miles, which is the Hyde Park of Florence, and surpasses for beauty even the Bois de Boulogne, so that we made a very good and delightful day of it. We purpose leaving this for Perugia on Monday, and arriving at Rome on Tuesday evening. The weather is beautiful, peas and beans out in blossom, and asparagus for dinner to-day. I forgot to mention that we obtained admission into the Royal Orange Conservatory belonging to the palace, filled with plants loaded with fruit.

Rome, April 9th.—Here we are at last, having travelled all night from Florence. We were rather afraid that we should have some difficulty in finding accommodation here, so thought it best to take the night train and arrive here in the morning, so as to have a whole day before us to look about. After inspecting four or five hotels and *Pensions*, and finding them nearly all full, we have settled upon the *Pension Anglais*. But I must go back to last Friday at Florence. In the morning we went again to the Laurentian Library, and then to the churches of *Santa Maria Novella* and *San Marco;* in the former there are some wonderfully fine frescoes by Ghirlandaio, and in both of them there are some very fine paintings by old masters : one gets rather confused amongst the number of churches. After this we went to the Academy of Fine Arts, which is chiefly composed of paintings dating from the 12th or 13th century down to the present time; some of the modern paintings by living artists are splendid. Everything shuts up at Florence at three o'clock, so after that hour we took a drive to a hill about a mile from Florence, called Bellosguardo, to get a view of the town, which lies very prettily along the valley of the Arno. The dome of the cathedral, which is higher than St. Paul's, stands out very well. We spent all Saturday morning till three o'clock in the Uffizi Gallery; this ranks the first for paintings in Florence. There is one room specially devoted to the old masters — Raphael, Michael Angelo, Cigoli, &c. After three o'clock we went into the Senate-house, where Admiral Pisano was being tried for mismanaging his fleet in the late war with Austria. But as we did not find out what was going on till the next day, we were not much the wiser. Sunday, we went to church, and drove to the Cascine in the afternoon. On Monday we went over the Royal Palace, and devoted the rest of the day to the pictures. There are a great many rooms in the palace, but mostly small in comparison with those at Paris. At about 8.0 p.m. we started for this place (Rome), and were glad enough to get here, at about ten this morning. We drove this afternoon to see the far-famed St. Peter's; my expectations were very great as regards the size and splendour, and I must confess they were more than fully realized. It is most magnificent. All the pictures are covered over now till Easter. The city of Rome itself is very poor; the streets, which are narrow and dirty, are not to be compared to Florence. On our way to St. Peter's we passed the castle of S. Angelo. The paintings at Florence surpass any I have ever seen, and I believe it to be the choicest collection in the world; altogether it is a most charming place. I have bought some stereoscopic views. The people of Italy are all born musicians, their very street cries are sung musically, and the language beautiful. It did my heart good this morning to hear at the railway station the old classical name, RŌMĀ, sung out with full Italian rotundity. Take another instance,—our blunt English word "Guide" is in French, "Commissionaire," but in the majestically flowing Italian, "Commissionario."

April 13th.—I am happy to say I am a great deal better, quite a different person from what I was when I left Genoa, where I began to think seriously of returning home. But this place suits me wonderfully;—there is a clearness in the atmosphere, and a bracing air with warm sun, which gives quite an elasticity and comfort to mind and body, and I do not remember any place which has agreed with me so well, and when I tell you presently what I do from day to day you will wonder.

I will now resume the thread of my narrative from Tuesday last. First of all, I suppose you will want to know something more of that wonder of the world, St. Peter's. We have now paid three visits to it—the last this afternoon, when we went over it leisurely. Upon the whole my impression of it is this, that, compared with S. Paul's, it is as inferior to it externally as a building, as it is superior to it internally for every thing. The colonnade and wide space in front also give it a vast advantage over S. Paul's. It is the various-coloured marbles, gilding, and painting which make such an addition to its architectural beauty inside, and give it a warmth and reality, as well as grandeur, in which S. Paul's falls vastly below it. The *Baldacchino*, or grand canopy, alone over the high altar cost nearly £22,000. Externally you see nothing but the façade and the dome (not so high as that of Florence cathedral) resting apparently upon it. I was of course much interested with the tomb erected at the expense of George IV. by Canova to the Stuart family. So much for a preface—now to the journal. On Wednesday morning we drove to the Capitol, so famous in the annals of Ancient Rome, and seated on one of her Seven Hills. The top is now covered with palaces, or what appears to be government offices, containing a museum of objects of interest connected with old Rome. Here is the most complete collection of ancient busts of the Emperors and other great men of old. That of Cicero struck me as very like Canning. Among the statuary is the famous

Dying Gladiator, the Amazon, the Antinous, the Fawn of Praxiteles, the prints of all which one has so often seen. The ancients beat us out and out in sculpture. Although I have seen to-day at S. Peter's the *chef d'œuvre* of Canova, it is not to be mentioned with the works of the Greeks and Romans. By the way, this reminds me that I forgot in my letter from Florence to mention that we saw there what, I suppose, stands almost unrivalled even among the relics of ancient sculpture—I mean the far-famed Venus de Medici, found in the Portico of Octavia, erected by Augustus in Rome. It was taken by Napoleon I. to Paris, but restored after 1815. In the Capitol are also a large collection of paintings, but they are secondary to those in the Vatican, which we have seen to-day. We next visited the Mamertine prisons, one of the few existing works of the Kingly period of Rome. Most horrible places they are, and here it was that S. Peter was confined by order of Nero. They show you the pillar to which he was bound, and the fountain which miraculously sprang up to enable him to baptize his jailors. This lies on the declivity of the Capitol. Near the base of the Capitol is the Arch of Septimius Severus, and here we stood among the ruins of old Rome, with columns of exquisite workmanship standing in solitude. These belonged to the temples which abounded there. Then we started up the old Forum Romanum, where we found a vehicle, and proceeded to the celebrated and interesting Arch of Titus, of white marble, erected to commemorate his conquest of Jerusalem, and on which I saw engraven the immense golden candlesticks from the Jewish temple and the silver trumpets, as parts of his spoil. Thence to the Arch of Constantine, a magnificent structure, and the most perfect of the architectural works of Ancient Rome. Next to the Colosseum. This struck me with amazement indeed;—only imagine an amphitheatre capable of containing 87,000 spectators! It was begun by Vespasian, and it is said that many thousand captive Jews were employed in its erection. Here it was that S. Ignatius and the many thousand Christian martyrs were thrown to the wild beasts. Here, too, were the gladiatorial combats.

Thursday.—We went first to the Capitol again, for the purpose of ascending the tower, which we could not do the day before, for want of an order from the senator. After a great deal of trouble and delay we at last obtained one, and were amply repaid, for here is the most perfect and magnificent view of Rome, as she *was* and *is*, of all the surrounding country and of the distant Sabine and other hills. Here we saw the Seven Hills—the site and ruins of the Palace of the Cæsars (of which more presently)—all the great buildings—the Campagna, &c. After this we went to find out the famous Tarpeian Rock, which is near the foot of the Capitol, and after some difficulty we found it, and had views of it in two different spots. The Rock is now built over, but its sides remain, only the earth is so much raised that thirty feet have been taken off the original height. It is still, however, very high. As Thursday is the only day for seeing the site and remains of the Palace of the Cæsars (lately purchased by the Emperor of the French), we went there next. And here we had the extreme good fortune to meet with a gentleman and lady from our hotel, waiting to join a party by appointment, who were to be conducted over the whole by a learned antiquarian resident here, so we asked permission to join. The party were all Scotch except a clergyman and ourselves. With the benefit of our conductor's explanations to the party, we had a great treat indeed. He showed us the site of the old Rome of Romulus where we stood, and which did not cover two-thirds of the space of the Palace of the Cæsars which occupied the whole Palatine Hill, now one and a half mile in circuit, and extended far beyond. The site of the two gates of the little city of Romulus was shown. The present accession of knowledge on all points of antiquarian interest, connected with the palace of the Cæsars, is due to the Emperor of the French, who has employed a distinguished archæologist to make excavations and explorations, which have brought to light recently much that was before unknown. The Palatine Hill before the time of the Emperors belonged to the great families in Rome, and Cicero, Clodius, &c. had their houses in it. It then passed into the hands of Augustus, who erected the first palace; this was added to by Tiberius and afterwards by Caligula. We walked along the Clivus Victoriæ, where the triumphal processions passed with the spoils to be laid up in the Capitol;—there was the place of abode of the vestal virgins, and where the holy fire was kept. But the most interesting part was that built by Augustus, where all the rooms were shown, particularly the Academia, where the Emperor sat in his tribune while the author, such as Virgil or Horace, recited his compositions to the judges who sat around,—all these seats still exist. It was during the month of April, according to Pliny, that these recitations took place daily. From thence we looked down on the Circus Maximus, which lies between the Palatine and Aventine hills, where the games were celebrated. Then there was the Triclinium, or Banqueting

Hall, and the Nympheum adjoining, with a large elegant fountain, by which the air was cooled and scented, that passed into the Triclinium, a most luxurious place; together with several of the rooms. But the most interesting of all was the Basilica, or Hall of Justice, which must have been the very place where S. Paul stood before Nero, when he was acquitted. That part of the marble balustrade, which separated the judicial seat from the place where the prisoner stood, is still left. So I took the opportunity of sitting in the seat of the Cæsars, and standing in the footsteps of S. Paul; the Emperor's seat being evident in every room. Two thousand of the Prætorian Guard were kept in this palace, and we visited the part where they were lodged, and on the walls were some drawings which showed there were Christians among them, for there was a ship (the ancient emblem of the church), and a fish (that of Christ), and His Name could be partly decyphered. Altogether it was a very great treat, and before we left, some of the party agreed to go together to visit the Colosseum the same evening by moonlight (which is much the best time to see it), an order being first obtained. We then drove with two of the party under the Arches of Titus and Constantine along the famous Via Appia to the Baths of Caracalla. It was by this Via Appia that S. Paul entered Rome, some of his nation having gone to meet him, as it is written, "as far as Appii Forum," which is about forty miles off. These mighty ruins are next in wonder to the Colosseum itself. On our way home we drove along the dusty road in the Circus Maximus, and I quoted, as we rolled along, the lines of Horace—

> "Sunt quos curriculo pulverem Olympicum
> Collegisse juvat."

At eight o'clock our party started to visit the Colosseum by moonlight. We were all, except ourselves, Scotch people, who had obtained an order. It is impossible to describe the exquisite appearance of this magnificent ruin by the soft light and shade of the half moon (the best to see it by), while a perfect stillness reigned over the whole scene. While we were gazing on the exterior, we heard voices of singing within, and supposed it to be some Italian service, as there is a pulpit inside in which a Friar preaches every Friday. On being admitted by the sentinal, we observed a party in the centre of the area singing most beautifully, men and women, under a wooden cross, which stands there,—still we supposed they were Italians, but judge of my emotions when I drew near and heard ascending from beneath this cross, in the sweetest notes of a kind of anthem, the words in English, "O

Lamb of God, that takest away the sins of the world," and "Christ, have mercy upon us," &c. We paused, and were awe-struck,—the deep stillness and solemnity of the scene—the associations of the place—the very spot where S. Ignatius and so many Christian martyrs had been thrown to the lions—made it altogether the most interesting and impressive moment you can conceive. When the singing ceased, we walked up and enquired who they were. They said they were Americans, and had been singing the "Gloria in Excelsis." I detected the words from the American Communion Office, and went up to a gentleman in naval uniform, and asked if he was an Episcopalian. "Yes," he said, "and not only so, but I am a clergyman and chaplain of a man of war now lying off Naples." I expressed my great pleasure in meeting him, as being the first American Episcopalian I had ever met, and we talked about Bishop Cleveland Cox (whom he said he had known all his life), and Hopkins, and he then gave me his card, with an invitation to visit him on board his ship, if I went to Naples. As I said, our own party were Scotch, all Presbyterians, and some of them ministers, so they proposed to the Americans to sing something in which they could *all* join, and the first verse of the Old Hundreth was fixed on, which we all sang under the cross with Bishop Ken's

Doxology. The whole day was one of the most delightful and interesting I had ever spent.

Friday.—I must be brief in what I have to say. We passed the morning at the Vatican, where there is a wonderful museum of antiquities, chiefly sculpture, of which I will only mention the far-famed Apollo Belvidere, and the Belvidere Antinous, among the many hundreds we looked at. Another very interesting gallery contained a collection of early Christian inscriptions, taken from the catacombs. This day was a great day in Rome, for it was the annual celebration of the Pope's return from Gaeta, and when he had a remarkable escape with all his dignitaries, by the floor of the room where they were assembled, near the church of S. Agnes, giving way and precipitating them all to the floor below, whence they escaped unhurt. On this day His Holiness goes to the church of S. Agnes to offer his thanksgivings, and then reviews his troops. We meant to have seen both, but could only manage the former, and had to wait in the church an hour and an half before the Pope arrived. He went to a seat in the gallery, where I could only see half his head, while the Te Deum was being very well chanted. After service we stood by his carriage a long time to see him come out, till we could wait no longer; but just after we had started off, and were walking alone by the side of the road, the procession drove by, the Pope in a state carriage drawn by four splendid black horses. We took off our hats as he passed, and His Holiness extended his hand to us by way of benediction in return. In the evening we were two hours driving all over the city to see the illuminations, which were indescribably pretty, as the Romans particularly excel in them. This day (Saturday) we have spent in the Vatican and at S. Peter's. In the former were three pictures which surpass, if possible, all I have ever seen, put together. I have written to the Pope's Chamberlain, Mons. Talbot, to be presented, and called with the note, but as he was with His Holiness, did not see him. To-morrow we must be at S. Peter's at 7.30 a.m, to be in time for the first grand ceremony.

April 23rd.—My last was brought down to the Saturday night before Palm Sunday. As I went to bed I said to the waiter, "*Nous déjeunerons à sept heures demain matin.*" To which he replied, "*Oui, Monsieur, tout le monde déjeunera à sept heures demain matin.*" So accordingly at 7.30 all the world and ourselves started for S. Peter's, where the service was to commence at 9.30. It was a clear and brilliant morning, and S. Peter's, as we drove up to it, looked its very best with the animated crowds repairing to it. That you may the better understand the nature of the ceremony, I must explain that this Basilica is in the form of a Latin Cross, and that in the centre of the cross stands the High Altar, beneath which repose the remains of the Apostles Peter and Paul, and round the space by which you descend below, ninety-three brass lamps are suspended, which are kept burning night and day. The area from behind the High Altar to the upper part of the cross is called the Pontifical chapel, at the upper end of which is the Tribune, where is placed the Papal Throne, which is a bronze chair inclosing (it is said) the identical wooden Episcopal chair used by S. Peter and his successors. In the space on each side of the High Altar are erected temporary raised seats for ladies, who have tickets (and none others are admitted), and these must be all dressed in black, without bonnets and only with veils on their heads, so that there is no opportunity for display. Gentlemen, too, must all appear in dress coats, and none others are admitted above half way up the nave. None enter the Pontifical chapel but those who take part in the ceremonies, except that there are temporary seats for royal princes on one side and their families and suite, and on the other for the Corps Diplomatique and their ladies and attendants. I should have said, that the above regulations as to dress apply to all the ceremonies of the Holy Week at S. Peter's and the Sistine chapel, including Easter Day. There is only standing room for gentlemen, and you may imagine what it was to have to stand from 7.30 to 1.0, but the crowd around you afford great support. After we had been there some little time, the Swiss Guards were marched up the Basilica in curious mediæval costume, with tall halberts in their hands, answering to our Yeomen of the Guard or Beefeaters. They took their stations so as to prevent the crowd from pressing into the open space behind the High Altar, and as I managed to get first behind one of them I had a capital front place, and got protected as well. After a little while the *Guardia Nobile* marched up the Basilica, about thirty or forty. These are the Pope's Body-Guard, and are composed entirely of the nobility of Rome. They were in splendid uniform, corresponding with our Horse Guards, and took their station on each side of the Pontifical chapel in two ranks, wearing their helmets after the old Roman type and with drawn swords. As the time drew on, the Corps Diplomatique and other grandees in splendid court-dresses, and glittering with orders and decorations, made their appearance, handing the ladies to their seats, so that the scene was altogether much like that of the House of Lords before the Queen's arrival, save the appearance of the ladies, which forms the gayest part of the latter. Bye and bye, the hum of voices was hushed into a deep silence, as an immense procession of ecclesiastics walked up the nave, consisting of cardinals, archbishops, bishops, abbots, &c., with their mitres on, and other persons connected with the Papal Court. The most conspicuous for the grandeur of their dress were some oriental bishops with their handsome mitres and long black beards. Here for the first time I saw the famous Cardinal Antonelli, whom I have often seen since. He is, what we call, the prime minister and has great influence in the Vatican. Last of all moved slowly up the Supreme Pontiff himself, seated on his *sedes gestatoria*, borne by poles on the shoulders of twelve *sediarii*, all attired in long red robes. The Pope wore a silver mitre, and passed within a yard or two of me, so that I had a good opportunity of studying his countenance. As he moved along, all either dropt on their knees or bent their bodies, while he kept extending his right arm in the form of benediction. His being carried in this way enables all to see him, otherwise being a short man he would be quite lost, as the whole Basilica seemed full. Every one remarks on the extreme amiability of his countenance, which, as to form and feature, resembles our photograph of him, but it entirely fails to give his expression. A great deal of time was occupied in going through the ceremonies at the Papal throne, the cardinals first doing homage, then followed the consecration and distribution of the palms, during all which services were being performed, and the choir of the Sistine chapel (the most exquisite you can possibly conceive) for this occasion brought to S. Peter's, singing "Hosanna in excelsis" and "Hosanna Filio David." After this the Pope was borne in procession down the Basilica, bearing a palm branch in his hand, and followed by all who had received palms, bearing them in their hands, the choir chanting all the time. Some ceremony takes place at the entrance door, and the Pope is then borne back to his throne. Then followed a celebration of high mass by a cardinal priest, during which the chapters relating to the Passion were chanted, the Pope having previously retired, as this service lasted about two hours, but he returned privately, and at a certain part left his throne and knelt at a faldstool before the high altar, uncovered. This, I believe, was at the passage recording the death of our Lord. At the conclusion, the Pope was carried again down the Basilica, with the same procession, followed by the *Guardia Nobile*, to whom the military word of command was given in the cathedral. After leaving his *sedes gestatoria*, he walked up part of one of the naves, myself close behind him, and retired to the Vatican. I have been somewhat explicit in this, as it was the first of the ceremonies I had witnessed, and it was not over till one o'clock. The union of the temporal and spiritual sovereignties gave the whole a strange appearance to an English eye, as it was such a combination of things civil, military, and ecclesiastical in a church,—still it was very imposing. I had abundance of opportunity of seeing the Pope, who at one time appeared very much worn and weary. He is the picture of what we should call "a fine old English gentleman"—light complexion, short gray hair, and plump in the face, with a little white skull cap, when uncovered. He sometimes changed one mitre for another, but did not wear the tiara. In the afternoon, we attended divine service at the English Chapel just outside the Porta del Popolo, as we are not allowed to worship within the walls. We afterwards started out separately, and I found my way to the Monte Pincio where are the public drives, walks, and gardens, and where all Rome seemed to have poured out, Sunday here being regarded as it is in all other parts of the continent—the shops open the greater part of the day. As the next grand church ceremony was not till Wednesday, we employed Monday and Tuesday in sight-seeing.

Monday, 15th.—We first went to the church of S. Pietro in Vinculis, to see the famous statue of Moses by Michael Angelo, of which it is said: "Men could build S. Peter's and men could build St. Paul's (another grand church in Rome), but none but Michael Angelo could make the statue of Moses." It is like all his other works, of colossal size, and full of life. Next—to the church of S. Martino de Monte, built on the site of an older one where was held by S. Sylvester the Councils of A.D. 324 and 330, when Arius, Sabellius, and Victorinus were condemned in the presence of Constantine, as represented in a large fresco. Here also lie the remains of S. Sylvester, S. Martin, and S. Francis Xavier. This we merely took on our way to the church of S. Prassede, where there was a special ceremony for this day. The father of SS. Prassede and Pudentiana was Pudens, the first person in Rome converted to Christianity by S. Paul, and said to be the husband of Claudia, who was a daughter of the British King Caractacus, and it was in his house that S. Paul lodged, and their tombs are here. But the principal interest attached to this church is the chapel in it called Orto del Paradiso, which derives its name from a small column of black and white marble, to which our Lord is said to have been bound at His scourging, and which was brought from Jerusalem A.D. 1223 by Cardinal Colonna. It also contains three of the thorns from the crown of thorns. I had a distinct view of both in the glass cabinet in which they are preserved. These are especially visited and venerated on Monday before Easter, and masses celebrated there. The pillar is not one that supported any building, but a mere round post. Next we visited the famous Basilica of Santa Maria Maggiore, the interior of which is considered the finest of its class in existence;—thence to that of the Lateran, which is the cathedral church of Rome, and where the Popes are crowned. It has this inscription on each side the entrance— " *Omnium urbis et orbis Ecclesiarum Mater et Caput*," and takes precedence of S. Peter's. It is well known for the Five General Councils that were held here, the last of which was the famous Council of Trent. The cloisters contain the episcopal throne of S. Sylvester—(his day in our calendar is December 31st)—also two columns of Pilate's house, a column said by tradition to have been split when the vail of the Temple was rent in twain, and the porphyry slab on which the soldiers cast lots for our Saviour's raiment;— also a miraculous altar-table of stone with a large hole in it, said to have been made by the consecrated wafer as it fell from the hands of a doubting priest. We then visited the Baptistry adjoining, and then the Scala Santa, consisting of twenty-eight marble steps, stated by tradition to have belonged to Pilate's house, and to have been the identical ones by which our Lord descended when He left the judgment hall. None are allowed to go up it except on their knees, and then to descend by another stairs. A lady and three Zouave soldiers were going up when we got there. We, however, with others, went up by the descending staircase, and on the top was a chapel containing a large collection of relics with an inscription over it: "*Non est in toto sanctior orbe locus.*" No woman is allowed to enter it, nor indeed into the Orto del Paradiso at S. Prassede, under pain of excommunication. In another chapel adjoining is a painting, said to be by S. Luke, of our Lord at the age of twelve. We next visited the museums of the Lateran, which are full of antiquities, and among others a number of Christian inscriptions brought from the Catacombs;—then to the famous church of San Clementi, one of the most ancient in Rome, and said to present one of the most perfect forms of the ancient Basilica. In it lie the remains of S. Clement, third bishop of Rome, and fellow labourer of S. Paul. It is a church full of interest to the antiquarian, but as I have bought a little book about it, I will not enlarge upon it now. We finished with the Baths of

Titus, on the site of what was originally the house and gardens of Mæcenas, on which Nero afterwards built his golden palace, converted by Titus into baths, lest the people should think that the emperors had acquired too much.

Tuesday.—Our first visit was to the church of Ara Cœli, erected on the site of the famous Temple of Jupiter Capitolinus, the pride and wonder of ancient Rome. It is approached by 124 marble steps from the ruins of the temple of Quirinus. Here it was that Gibbon says, as he sat musing amidst the ruins of the Capitol, the first idea suggested itself of writing the "Decline and Fall." It is called Ara Cœli from the altar erected here by Augustus, to commemorate the prophecy of the Cumean Sybil respecting the coming of our Saviour. But that which gives the church peculiar veneration with the Romans is the miracle-working figure of the Infant Saviour, called "*Santissimo Bambino*," on account of its powers in curing the sick, of which a friend had told us. We therefore inquired specially of the monks about this image, and were given to understand that it was gone to effect the cure of a sick person, and we could not see it until its return. But as they could only speak Italian, I waited till a priest came and conversed with him in Latin, when he confirmed what we understood from the monks, and said we could see it after three hours. We accordingly went to see some things we had overlooked in the Capitol, and when there heard the military bugle, and on looking out of the window A—— saw the soldiers presenting arms, as a little bundle was taken out of a handsome private carriage by a priest. This we had no doubt was the Bambino returned, so we went at once back to the church, and found it was so. It had been deposited in its iron safe in the chapel, and a monk came to show it us. He first lighted two tapers which he put on each side of the box, and after unlocking it, took off the folds in which it was wrapt, and exposed a little wooden image dressed up and covered with gems and precious stones, the offerings of the pious, with a gold crown on, also adorned with precious stones. The monk told us it was made of wood from the Mount of Olives, and the face painted by an angel. He reverently kissed the foot before putting it up again. In 1849 the Republican government made the monks a present of the Pope's state carriage for the use of the Bambino, but on the Pope's return it was restored. Thence we visited the ruins of the temple of Marcellus and the portico of Octavia (sister of Augustus), where the famous statue of the Venus de Medici was found;— then to the temple of Vesta—the arch of Janus

Quadriferus, and the arch of Septimius Severus in the Velabrum;—then to a very interesting piece of antiquity, the Cloaca Maxima, being a subterranean canal, built by Tarquinius Priscus, fifth King of Rome, as a sort of large common sewer from the city to the Tiber. It is still as firm as when its foundations were first laid;— then along the Via Appia to the Columbaria, which are immense subterranean excavations, the walls of which are pierced throughout with a sort of pigeon holes for receiving the urns containing the ashes of the dead in the time of the early Cæsars. There are inscriptions to each, containing the name and age, and several are mentioned as attached to the household of the Cæsars;—thence to the tomb of the Scipios spoken of by Cicero. It consists of long subterranean labyrinths in which some of the tombs still remain, the name of "Cornelius Scipio" being very plain. Next under the arch of Drusus (the oldest in Rome) to the church of S. Sebastian, from which a door opens leading to the catacombs, which we explored, each being furnished with a taper, and our guide taking several in his hand. They are vast and winding subterranean passages, and in them were pointed out to us the little chapels where the early Christians used to worship. Much of the interest is lost by the inscriptions having been removed and placed on the walls of the galleries in the Vatican and Lateran Museums, where we had seen them. From thence we went to the circus of Romulus, where the ancient chariot-races took place. This is the most perfect of the circuses that are left. Next we came to the tomb of Cæcilia Metella, an immense mausoleum, and one of the best preserved monuments about Rome, erected more than nineteen centuries ago to the memory of Cæcilia Metella, the wife of Crassus. We then drove about a mile further along the Via Appia, amidst ruins on every side, extending far and wide, making a scene of desolation, which it was mournful to behold. On our return we visited a temple of Bacchus, now converted into a farm-house, where there are three magnificent Corinthian columns stuck within its mud walls;—then a lovely, picturesque spot, said to be the fountains and grove of Egeria, where Numa held his nightly consultation with the Nymph. All this was accomplished before dinner, and in the evening we went to the performance of the "Stabat Mater" in the Palazzo Doria, which was very well done, the choir being amateurs. The "Cujus Animam" was very beautiful. This finished our day's work—and a pretty good one, but yet not so fatiguing as those of the subsequent days, which we devoted to religious ceremonies.

Wednesday.—In the morning we went about some commissions, and selected some photographs for ourselves, and at 2 p.m. started for the Sistine chapel, to secure places for the Nocturns or Tenebræ service at 4.30. After being kept waiting an hour outside before we were allowed to ascend the stairs, when I got to the door of the chapel from the Sala Regia, the Swiss Guard abruptly turned me back because I had my stick. I offered to throw it away, but still he would not let me in, so I retired a little and flung it to the other end of the hall, and then entered with the crowd, fearing that through the delay I had lost all chance of getting a good place. However, I managed as usual to get one, by squeezing behind one of the Swiss Guards, and so had one of the best front places. Still I had to stand till 4.30 before the service began, none but ladies and grandees having seats. The cardinals having entered in their dark violet robes, some psalms were chanted by the choir,— and here I may remark that both in the Sistine chapel and S. Peter's the music is all vocal, there being no organ in either. Afterwards came a most exquisite chant in four voices from the "Lamentations of Jeremiah," by Palestrina,—as an old gentleman at the hotel remarked to me, they were "songs without words," the sounds speaking to the heart, although the words could not be distinguished. Then followed more chanting of psalms and lessons, during which all the candles were gradually extinguished. Through the kindness of a gentleman standing next me, I was able to follow the chanting. Presently the Pope entered, and took his seat until the time came for the "Miserere;" he then left it and knelt at a faldstool before the altar with all the cardinals and their attendants kneeling behind him, during the whole time of the chanting of the "Miserere," or 51st psalm, which lasted half an hour, and was most exquisitely done. I confess that the scene was to me much more impressive than any thing the Sunday before. It was simply *Ecclesiastical*, and to see the head of two hundred millions of spiritual subjects with his cardinal princes behind him, kneeling for half an hour to the plaintive strains of that deeply-penitential psalm, before God's altar in his own little unadorned chapel, was a most moving and instructive sight. The opening of the "Miserere" was particularly touching.

Thursday.—We again repaired to the Sistine chapel, in time for high mass, at 11.0 a.m., in the presence of the Pope and Sacred College, at the close of which a procession was formed to the neighbouring Pauline chapel in the Vatican, in which the Pope carries the sacrament. He passed close to me, himself and the cardinals reciting in a low tone as they moved along. After this followed the Pontifical benediction *urbi et orbi* from the balcony in front of S. Peter's, which was also very impressive, but as this was still more so on Easter Day, I will reserve my description of it for the present. After this, we re-entered S. Peter's to see the ceremony of the Pope washing the feet of thirteen priests, as representatives of the Apostles, selected from every country. They all sat in a row on a high bench, and were dressed in white. The Pope having been invested with an apron, and assisted by two cardinal deacons, washes and wipes the feet of each, and kisses them. There was a very great crush to witness this, and one of the Zouave soldiers lifted his musket and threatened to hammer A——'s toes; but we left before it was over in order to get places in the banqueting-hall for the next ceremony. Here the crush and heat were terrific, but having once got in it was impossible to get out. However, we had an excellent view. There was a table most handsomely set out, at one side of which sat these same thirteen priests, whom the Pope served. First, he walked up and served each with a basin of soup—then with wine—and afterwards with two courses of fish and more wine. He was looking the picture of kindness and venerability, being uncovered, and a mere red cape over his white robes. After undergoing what we did, we were glad to get back and have a warm bath. The Pope appears to be personally loved and respected by all. He expends all he can for the benefit of the city, but there is a general feeling that it is only his own life that delays the revolution, and certainly nothing can be more inconvenient than the present relationship between the Italian and Roman Governments.

Good Friday.—We went to the morning service at the English church. Nothing has so much shocked my English sense of propriety since I have been here, as the mode in which this day is externally disregarded—shops all open and business going on just as usual. Here again extremes meet, and Edinburgh and Rome keep the day much alike. Not but there are special services in all the churches; and a large one, where I looked in to see the three hours' agony kept, was full of people. In the afternoon we went to a Tenebræ service at S. Peter's, during which the Pope came into the church to pray before the tomb of the Apostles, after which were exhibited in his presence from a balcony in the church, the sacred relics, namely, a part of the true cross and the *Volto Santo*, or handkerchief of S. Veronica, of which you know the legend. These were enclosed in a glass case with silver frame, so that it was impossible really to see them. Before the Pope came, we witnessed a curious ceremony — the Cardinal Grand Penitentiary in a seat holding a long gold wand in his hand, with which he touched every one who came to him on the head. "Murray" says, this is "to give absolution for mortal sins, which cannot otherwise be absolved;" but this I can hardly believe, as there appeared to be no confession or preparation: still as he sat to hear confessions the day before, the persons who came might be known to him. Apparently the people offered themselves promiscuously, but the touch of the wand without saying a word, was, at the least, a strange mode of giving absolution.

Saturday.—We went at 9.0 a.m. to attend an interesting service in an equally interesting place, a general ordination in the church of S. John Lateran, so famous in history, where the dogma of transubstantiation was decreed A.D. 1215. The ceremony began soon after we arrived, by a long procession entering the church chanting, and then walking all round the church, consisting of the cardinal vicar of Rome, wearing a splendid mitre with his crozier in his hand, attended by several priests and the candidates, to the number of sixty or seventy, all robed in white. When he reached the altar where the ordination was to take place, he knelt down before it, and all the candidates threw themselves prostrate on the ground behind him, and continued for some time in prayer in that posture, so that the floor was a sheet of white. This had a very impressive appearance. The service was a very long one, there being ordinations of acolytes, sub-deacons, deacons, and priests. The cardinal invested each with his particular vestment, the acolytes with the cotta, the sub-deacons with the dalmatica, the deacons with the stole, and the priests with the chasuble and maniple. The mode of ordaining the priests was far more impressive than ours, for instead of the bishop and two priests laying their hands all together, as with us, the bishop first laid both his hands on each, and afterwards the archdeacon and other priests went round to each, as they were kneeling, and laid their hands on them severally. There was a mass and communion afterwards, but after standing three hours we left before it was over. In the evening we went to the hospital of *Trinità de Pellegrini* to see the washing of the feet of the pilgrims by the cardinals, nobility, and other chief men in Rome, and waited on by them afterwards at supper. This was a very curious scene. It had been done on Wednesday and Thursday evenings as well, and this was the last evening. The ladies of Rome did the same to female pilgrims, but this we were not permitted to see. The pilgrims must have come from a distance of more than sixty miles and brought certificates from their bishops with them. There were four hundred altogether, including eighty women. You never saw such a set of ragamuffins. All who waited on them were robed in a long red dress, helped to take the dirty shoes and stockings off, washed, wiped, and kissed their feet, and then helped to put the shoes and stockings on—all joining, the whole time, in reciting some words in a low tone. I stood by an old cardinal and saw him do it all. When this was over, they went to the dining-room, where these grandees waited on the pilgrims; but we did not remain after the plate of soup was served round. This finished the much-talked-of Holy Week. There were other ceremonies which we did not attend, and merely selected the more important, and such as were within our power. And now, how shall I find words to describe Easter Sunday! Much must be left to your imagination, and even that will fail you. I was awoke at day-break by the guns of the castle of S. Angelo booming over the city. This was soon followed by the clatter of church bells for early masses, and at 7.30 we started for S. Peter's. The Swiss Guards were on this occasion in steel armour, and the *Guardia Nobile* in splendid scarlet uniform instead of blue, which they wore before, and the pillars of S. Peter's were hung with red drapery. I got, as before, behind one of the Swiss Guards in an excellent front place. About 9.30 the long procession of cardinals, prelates, and other dignitaries came slowly up the church with splendid mitres and robes, the blue violet ones of Lent being exchanged for the white and yellow ones of Easter. After them came the Pope in his *sedes gestatoria*, wearing his tiara which was covered with jewels, and extending his right arm in benediction, as before. The silver trumpets played him up the nave. There was a great deal of ceremony, as on Palm Sunday, after he was seated, the cardinals doing homage and kissing his hand, or rather the ring on it, and the others kissing the gold cross in front of his white shoe, which is vulgarly called "kissing the Pope's toe." On this day the Pope celebrates high mass himself, before which the office of Tierce was sung by the Sistine choir, the music on this day being said to be the most beautiful in the whole range of sacred music. The Pope chanted the service in a fine clear voice, assisted by the choir, and when he came to the elevation of the Host, I never shall forget, and cannot possibly describe the few minutes that followed. S. Peter's was full, and all knelt or bowed in deep silence, when at that instant

the silver trumpets were heard filling the dome
and all the avenues of that magnificent temple
with the sweetest and richest sounds' you can
possibly conceive; it was quite unearthly, and one
seemed for the time in Paradise. The trumpeters
could not be seen, but the sound seemed to come
from the dome. As soon as they ceased, all rose
up from their posture of adoration. After the
conclusion of the service, the Pope was carried
from his throne to the middle of the nave, where
he alighted and knelt at a faldstool before the
altar and tomb of the Apostles, in private prayer.
He then re-ascended his portable seat and with
his tiara on his head was borne out of the church,
the fans of ostrich and peacocks' feathers being
carried on each side. But when I left S. Peter's,
how shall I describe the sight that burst upon
me! You must understand that beyond the
colonnade is a very large open space, called
the *Piazza de San Pietro*, and that from the
commencement of the colonnade there is a
gradual ascent to S. Peter's. When I left the
church, I looked down on the whole of this vast
open space filled—and not only so, but the roofs
and windows of the houses beyond, containing
occupants, all dressed in their best, with the
most perfect order and decorum, waiting for the
appearance of the Pope at the balcony in front
of S. Peter's. It was about a quarter of an

hour before he came, borne on his *sedes*, as before, and wearing the tiara. The benediction is rather lengthy, and concludes with the words: "*Et benedictio Dei Omnipotentis, Patris, Filii et Spiritus Sancti descendat super vos, et maneat semper. Amen.*" Until he comes to those words, he continues sitting and intoning the Benediction from a book held before him. This he did with a fine clear voice, which could be heard probably over the whole of the vast space before him. But at the words "*Et benedictio,*" he rises, makes the three signs of the cross at the words "*Patris et Filii et Spiritus Sancti,*" then spreads out his hands towards heaven, and lets them fall over the people at the words "*descendat super vos.*" At the instant it is over, the guns of S. Angelo send forth their salvos, the people raise a shout, the military bands strike up, and the bells of S. Peter's clatter, so that the contrast between the deep interval of stillness, when all were either standing uncovered or kneeling, and this sudden burst of joy is very striking. The Pope remains a few minutes after giving the Benediction, then rises again and gives another, but without pronouncing the above words, and retires. A—— and I soon afterwards met at the entrance, and sat down on the top step, and gazed on the scene, as the people were departing with the almost endless cortège of state carriages among them, and

F

we both said that nothing could exceed it for magnificence in the world. You may imagine the number of people, when I tell you that Rome was never known to be so full of English and Americans, come here for the occasion, and the authorities compute them at 30,000. These, of course, were all there, to say nothing of other foreigners, besides the population of Rome, and the multitudes that had flocked in from the country; for on this day every shop is shut, and there was an entire suspension of work. They took an immense time in dispersing, but all was done in the most perfect quietness and order. After this I felt that I had seen and heard enough, and that all other scenes in my life would pale before it. In the afternoon we attended the English Church service, and in the evening went out to see the famous illumination of S. Peter's. There are two—the first, called the silver illumination, begins at seven, and consists of 5,900 lanterns, and the second, the golden one, at eight, of 6,800. Each is done instantaneously, so as to appear the work of enchantment, and as this blaze of light to the highest point of the cupola stands out against the dark sky, the appearance is most splendid. The instantaneous change from the silver to the golden at eight o'clock was very striking. We had a capital view from an eminence near.

Easter Monday.—After attending service at the English church, and writing a great part of this letter, we took a carriage to the famous church of *San Paolo fuori le Mura*, second only to S. Peter's itself; it is some way beyond the walls. Under the high altar was at one time the burial place of S. Paul, and before the Reformation the Kings of England were protectors of this church, and the shield bearing the abbot's arms is surrounded by the ribbon of the Order of the Garter, with the words "*Honi soit, &c.*" It is a most magnificent church, and has one of its altars entirely of malachite with gold ornaments. In the evening we attended that splendid display of fireworks on the Monte Pincio, for which Easter Monday is so famous in Rome. I will only say that it was most wonderful, and surpasses all description.

Easter Tuesday.—We went over the picture galleries in the Palazzo Borghese, the Palazzo Doria, and the Palazzo Spada, the latter famous for containing the identical statue of Pompey, at the foot of which "great Cæsar fell," and which, Shakespeare says, "all the while ran blood." You may imagine how intensely we gazed upon it. It is eleven feet high, and presents a noble figure, with the stern majesty of the old Roman strongly marked in the countenance. Afterwards, we saw the pictures in the gallery of S. Luke and the convent of S. Leonardo, which the monks showed us over—and the Pantheon.

April 25th.—I brought my journal down to yesterday in my letter to M——. To-day we have been over the Quirinal Palace and another palace. I have looked over some good photographs on a large scale, which will be sent off to London, and a letter to me at Dursley will be sent from thence, when they arrive, which must be answered by ordering them to be forwarded to Dursley. I forgot in my letter yesterday to say, that on Good Friday afternoon I attended a mass celebrated by an Armenian bishop, according to the form of their church.

April 26th.—I omitted to say, that on Easter Eve the custom is in every parish in Rome, for the Curate to enter every house and give his benediction. I happened to be in the passage when he entered in his robes, with two attendants, and walked upstairs. I waited till he came down, and asked him a question or two. I know from good authority that after the Pope had given his Easter Day Benediction, he remarked that he believed it would be his last. To-day we have visited the crypt of S. Peter's, and seen the Tomb of the Apostles, also the tombs of the Stuarts, with their full regal titles over them;—also seen a white marble column of exquisite workmanship in S. Peter's, brought from the Temple of Jerusalem, and said to be part of Solomon's Temple, against which (it is said) our Saviour leant, when He taught the people. The four bronze pillars to the canopy of the High Altar are made after its model. Afterwards we went to the Vatican Library, and saw there the Presentation Copy to the Pope by Henry VIII. of his book against Luther, with his autograph signature attached,—also an autograph letter of Anne Boleyn. I have had no answer to my letter to the Pope's Chamberlain, and no wonder, for I see by the papers that he had to receive six hundred, who were presented to him last week, in addition to all the public ceremonies.

Naples, May 2.—You will, I know, be glad to hear that we are safely here, and have hitherto escaped the brigands. My last letter was written the day before we left Rome, last Friday. We had a pleasant journey here next day, in company with a Canadian party, who had just returned from a tour through Palestine, including Jerusalem, &c., which was very agreeable. The first part of the journey out of Rome was full of objects of interest, as the railway was parallel with the Via Appia, marked by its line of ruined sepulchres, and also with the ancient Roman Aqueduct, the Alban hills forming a very fine boundary to the scene. We passed the famous monastery of Monte Casino, more like a palace than a convent, the grandest and most ancient monastic establishment in Europe, being founded by, and the residence of, S. Benedict. After we got into the Italian territory, we observed persons stationed at short intervals along the line, as a sort of telegraph to give warning, if necessary, of the brigands. The latter part of the journey, for about twenty miles before we reached Naples, was through a most rich and luxuriant country, far surpassing anything I have seen in England, all the land being under cultivation, and the trees hung with festoons of vines, the wheat also being full grown, and looking remarkably fine. We arrived here soon after 6.0 p.m., but it was more than half-an-hour before we could leave the station, where we were beset by a crowd of people offering their services, that is, rogues who would run away with one's luggage, and by beggars. We drove to the Hotel de Russe, where we are comfortably quartered. I should have said, that the whole line of country from Rome to this is very picturesque and beautiful, the snow-capped Apennines forming a fine object during much of the way. On Sunday, we attended morning and afternoon service at the English church, and on our way back in the afternoon, took a drive along the Chiaja and the road beyond out of the city, which forms the fashionable drive, and from whence we had a fine view of the far-famed Bay and the city, which certainly did not disappoint the highest expectation. The streets are crowded with people, who seem to live out of doors, but the greater part are a dirty, lazy set, lying about and spoiling the charm which Nature has so lavishly bestowed on this beautiful spot. We met at our hotel some of our old Roman friends, who had planned an excursion to Vesuvius next day, and allowed us to join them. Accordingly, we were called at 3.30 on Monday morning, and between 4.0 and 5.0 a.m., a large party of us (gentlemen and ladies) started in carriages for Resina, a town about four miles off, at the foot of Vesuvius, and beneath which Herculaneum lies buried. Here we engaged guides, with whom we started on ponies and mules, which took us at a walking pace along a most rough and uneven track over fields of lava, till we reached the bottom of the cone. W—— says in a letter, that I speak only of the beauties of Art, and wants to know if I have seen none of Nature. He may be satisfied when I tell him that the wonders of Nature on this one day far surpassed all those of Art which we have ever seen. On each side of our rugged track were vast square miles of lava, that is, of molten rock in enormous folds and wreaths, presenting a most marvellous sight, just as though the earth had been disembowelled and cast up her entrails on the surface. It was awful to think that all this had been poured out from the central furnace of the earth, for it had all the appearance of having just flowed over and hardened. This ride to the foot of the cone was six miles, and very fatiguing. We had all then to dismount and ascend the cone, how we could. This was another hour's work. All the gentlemen, except myself, were young men, and of course enjoyed the fun, a great part of which was to assist the ladies, some of whom were strapped round the waist and hauled up by the guides with the assistance of the gentlemen. The cone is very steep and is formed of lava, stones and cinders, thrown up during the eruptions, which add much to the difficulty of climbing. Myself and one of the ladies engaged a portable chair each, and were carried by poles resting on the shoulders of four men. This was dreadfully nervous work, for as there was no sure footing for the men, the chair was constantly reeling from side to side, and at one time it came down with me, and then the awful height, with the clouds, sea, and land beneath us, added greatly to the terror of the journey. I was exclaiming "*prenez garde,*" and my bearer "*pas de danger, Monsieur,*" all the way. I would not undergo it again for a great deal. However, we were amply repaid when we reached the crater. The smoke was rising from many parts, and some eggs were cooked on the soil, of which we partook. Every thing here wore a different appearance from the sides of the cone we had ascended, for all the surface was of a yellow and green colour, from the stones of sulphur with which it was covered. We walked round some parts of the edge of the crater, to get a sight of Pompeii. The view was magnificent — on one side the range of the Apennines, and on the other the Mediterranean, with the beautiful Bay of Naples, and the city and populous country about it. The descent was of course much more rapid than the ascent, but not less frightful to me, for I was carried backward in the chair, and occasionally round some terrific turnings. We then remounted our animals, and had the same dreary, wearisome ride to take over the lava, back to the town of Resina. Along the latter part of the ride, the lava had been brought into cultivation, and a wine called "Lacryma Christi" is made from the vines which grow on it. We had some on the top of Vesuvius, and it was delicious. We got back to Naples about three o'clock, all very tired, and glad to get some rest before dinner.

Tuesday.—We joined an American gentleman and two young Portuguese in the hire of a carriage, to take us to Herculaneum and Pompeii. The former does not possess much interest, except to the antiquarian, as it is buried in lava under the town of Resina; no further excavations are being made for fear of the surface falling in, and all the objects of interest have been removed and placed in museums. It was destroyed by lava at the same time as Pompeii, in the year 79, and was discovered about 100 years ago in the same manner as Pompeii, by sinking a well. The only part to be seen, and that by the aid of candles, in its subterraneous state is the Theatre, the different parts of which have been brought to light by the excavations. Thence we had a most dusty and disagreeable drive to Pompeii, than which there can be nothing more interesting. This was destroyed, not by lava, but by showers of stones and ashes from Vesuvius, and consequently is not so imbedded in hard rock as Herculaneum. About one third of the city has been excavated, and the works are still in progress, the Italian Parliament having voted £1000 a year towards the expense, which is much too little. Here is the city with its streets and houses, just as it was when it was suddenly destroyed, with some figures of human beings encased in the fatal shower. Many of the most valuable curiosities have been removed to the museum here, which we saw yesterday. The Forum and other public buildings and the Amphitheatre are particularly perfect. This expedition occupied the whole day, and I long to pay another visit. All yesterday we spent in the museum and seeing the church of S. Martine, second only to S. Peter's at Rome. To-day we go to Sorrento, and return to-morrow, and on Monday we go with a lady and her daughter to Baiæ. The air is cool, mornings and evenings, and I am getting stronger every day.

Naples, May 7th.—My last was brought down to Wednesday in last week, which no doubt has now been received. The next day (Thursday) we started by train to Castellamare, and thence by carriage for Sorrento, a most beautiful spot, and a favourite resort of all travellers; also well known in classic history. We put up at a quiet *Pension* in the loveliest part of the place, with rooms looking to the sea. The same afternoon we took a drive of four miles to Massa, and ought to have crossed over to Capri in a boat, but we heard so much of the sea-sickness of a party who had made the attempt the day before, that we did not follow their example, which I am, nevertheless, rather sorry for. Next morning we started, I on a donkey and A—— on foot, up a tremendous hill to a place called the Deserto, and thence to the village of S. Agatha. From the top of this hill we had a most splendid view of land and sea scenery,—the Mediterranean with its fine deep blue, including the Bay of Naples, and all the surrounding coast, and the Gulf of Salerno with a fine mountain range. We had a most lovely drive back to Castellamare the same evening, and thence to Naples by train. We fell in on that day with some ladies of our Vesuvian party, and others whom we had before met, which made it very agreeable. These little excursions give us the opportunity of seeing something of Italian country life, which is one of the most primitive you can conceive—at least in South Italy,—women doing mason's work with the men, &c. The country round is most rich and picturesque, the slopes cultivated with the vine and olive, and the vale with orange groves. As we went through one, I had two oranges from the tree, and never tasted anything more delicious. My plan was to have gone to Amalfi, and from thence to Sorrento, but I was deterred, from what I heard of the brigands.

Saturday.—We finished off the museum, intending to have paid afterwards another visit to Pompeii, but there was so much to interest us in the former, we could not afford the time, so, after visiting the cathedral, A—— went for a drive with a Marlbro' man, and I took a warm bath. I forgot to mention in my last our visit to the castle of S. Elmo—a large fortress adjoining the town, and I also omitted to enclose some "maiden hair" which I picked from the walls of Pompeii, and now enclose all I have left of it.

Sunday.—This was a remarkable day. You have often heard and read (I dare say) of the Liquefaction of the Blood of S. Januarius. I remember reading an article on it in a No. of the *Union Review*. It is the greatest religious festival in Naples, and I was very glad to be here at the time. There are three of them in the year—in May, September, and December. That you may properly understand it, I will make a little preface of its history. S. Januarius is the patron saint of Naples, and the cathedral is dedicated to him. When he was exposed in the third century to be devoured by lions in the amphitheatre of Puteoli, they prostrated themselves before him and became tame. I was at the amphitheatre yesterday, and saw the place where he was confined, on which there is now a little chapel to his memory. This miracle is said to have converted so many to Christianity, that, by order of the Roman Emperor, the saint was decapitated. The sentence was executed at Solfatara A.D. 305. I was there also yesterday, and saw the monastery with its church, erected in

1580 by the Neapolitans on the spot where he is said to have suffered martyrdom. The body remained buried at Puteoli until the time of Constantine, when it was removed to Naples by S. Severus the bishop, and deposited in a church. At the time of this removal, the Roman lady, who is said to have collected the blood at the time of the martyrdom, took it in two bottles to S. Severus, in whose hands it is said to have immediately melted. In 1497 the body of the saint, which had been removed to Benevento in the ninth century, was brought again to Naples with great solemnity and deposited in the cathedral. The two phials, which are said to contain the blood collected by the lady, are kept in an iron safe, and fixed in the wall behind the high altar in the cathedral, and secured by two locks, one key being kept by the municipal authorities, and the other by the bishop. It so happened that I had a first-rate opportunity of seeing and examining the whole minutely, from the very first to the last, through the kind assistance of a Roman Catholic lady, a friend of a lady in our hotel, to whom I had mentioned the subject, and who, like me, was very anxious to witness the ceremony. This R. C. lady obtained from the authorities permission for us to go, where only the most privileged are admitted. So on Sunday morning, between seven and eight a.m. we started, a party of five of us (including the R. C. lady) for the cathedral, which was then filling fast. After securing our places we had to wait about an hour, during which masses were being celebrated. We were then admitted to the narrow space between the high altar (which, by the way, is a splendid one of richly-carved silver) and the iron safe with its two folding doors. Bye and bye, the bishop and the prince (as he is called), that is, the head of the civil authorities in the city, came with due ceremonial, each with his key, and unlocked the safe. They first took out a large silver bust of the saint, and carried it to be deposited by the altar. This is said to contain his real head. During this little delay our party had full opportunity of examining the phials, one by one. They were suspended in a glass case in the safe, one large and the other small, and my attention was fixed on the former. It had a substance which had the appearance of congealed blood, with which it was about three parts filled, the empty part of the bottle being lowermost as it remained suspended, so that it was quite clear that what was in the upper part was in a solid state, as it did not move. I went close to it and examined it most minutely. The bishop then returned and took the phials in the glass case out of the safe, and presented it to such as chose, that they might kiss it. He then carried it in front of the altar, to exhibit it to all the congregation. I followed him, and did not take my eye off the bottle for a moment. He then walked with it, backwards and forwards, before the altar, holding it up before all the people, and allowing any to come as near as they could for about ten minutes, but the substance still continued unmoved, being suspended in the upper part of the bottle. During all this time, and indeed before it began, there was a tremendous clatter of voices in the cathedral, chiefly from a set of old women who claim to be of the family of the saint, and sit in a privileged place, and as soon as mass is over, begin reciting their Pater Nosters, Aves and Credos with the intention of supplicating the saint to effect the liquefaction. If it does not take place soon, their entreaties turn to abuses, with which they go on until the liquefaction begins, and then all is applause. I do not know that they used any abusive words on Sunday, because it was only about ten minutes before the liquefaction took place, and as soon as it was seen, there was a great burst of joy—the organ struck up—chanting began—and the people sobbed aloud, the tears rolling down their cheeks for joy. The reason of this is that the miracle never fails, without some grievous calamity befalling the city. The substance began to move quite gradually, and at last, freely, so that as the bishop moved the phial up and down, the blood flowed either way. I did not take my eye off it once, but kept examining it with my opera glass, which is a very good one. Any one might go up and look at it, and most of the people did, for the purpose of kissing the casket. Our R. C. friend was in an ectasy of delight. She is a very ardent and warm-hearted person— has been twice a widow—and a pervert of about five or six years standing, and this was the first miracle she had ever seen. She appealed to us all by turns, and was very pressing upon A——. She had been presented to the Pope, with a vast number of others, in Holy Week, and cried so much all the time, that His Holiness was obliged to tell her not to cry so. I had a sharp skirmish with her—not that I denied the miracle, for after all, granting it to be one, it proves nothing, for it is not pretended that it supports any doctrine, and when the liquefaction first took place, according to the tradition, in the reign of Constantine, it was before Popery was born or thought of. I told her it was much more difficult to prove that it was the blood of S. Januarius than it was to prove the fact of the liquefaction. On each occasion of the festival, the miracle is repeated every day for seven days, and the day we went was the second. But an old and very

Low Church clergyman from our hotel had gone the first day, only not in time to see the liquefaction, that is, not the act of the substance turning from a solid to a liquid state—he merely saw it in the latter, so he came back and said it was "monstrous." However, next morning he followed our party, being determined to see the whole, so he was there all the time, and got nearly as close as we were—but when we met at luncheon afterwards, he could only say it was "most extraordinary." Greatly must he have been disappointed at not being able to detect "the trick," as they call it. This clergyman I had met at Rome and Sorrento, where we were at the same hotel, and he preached in the English church at Naples that same Sunday afternoon, and included in his sermon, among those who were not on their way to heaven, all English, Americans, and Scotchmen who had gone to S. Peter's at Rome on Easter Sunday morning, because they had broken the sabbath by going sight-seeing; forgetting that he had done the same that very morning in a much truer sense. I could tell you a great deal of the strange deeds of this same clergyman, but must return to my narrative. After the ceremony of the liquefaction was over, we adjourned to the sacristy, where we were privileged to see all the ornaments and jewels that had been presented to S. Januarius, to be worn on the silver bust, which contains his head. They were all presents from crowned heads and princes, the last, and one of the most costly, being from Victor Emmanuel. I should scarcely think any monarch in Europe possessed jewels more handsome and valuable, the mitre also was covered with precious stones. All these are put on the bust in processions on these festivals, one of which was to take place next day, but we did not go. In the papers of the Camden Society there is an interesting account of the private exhibition of the miracle in 1696, by Lord Perth, chancellor of Scotland at the fall of the Stuarts. The only importance attached to the miracle in Naples is the effect in the way of calamity to the city, in the event of its failing—a very harmless notion, which one may very well leave them quietly to enjoy, but I am quite sure from all I have seen and heard since I left England, that it is a most dangerous thing to disturb the long-established traditions of a people. Italy is now flooded with infidelity from this very cause. What it wanted was a good system of education, which must be a very gradual process, and in the meantime the choice of evils is to let things be as little disturbed as possible. The French Revolution ought to be a sufficient warning on this point. But to return from this little episode. We came back from the cathedral in time for the English church morning service, where we went again in the afternoon, and afterwards strolled in the beautiful gardens adjoining the sea, with some of our lady friends whom we happened to meet. The subject of the liquefaction has been much discussed of course at the table in our hotel, but as it consisted chiefly of the theories of persons who had not witnessed it, and which I pretty well shut up when I had a chance, particularly when I was coolly asked if I saw how "the trick was done," I need not say any more about it.

Monday.—We made an engagement with our friends, Mrs. and Miss M——, to go together to Baiæ, Cumæ, and other intermediate places, the most classic soil in all Italy. First, we visited the tomb of Virgil, for in or near Naples he lived and died, and composed his admirable works, and it was from Naples that he went to meet Augustus at Athens, which gave occasion to Horace to compose that beautiful ode, containing the exquisite line, "*Et serves animæ dimidium meæ.*" From thence we went to Puteoli, now called Pozzuoli, which, you remember, was the place where S. Paul landed after his dangerous voyage in the Mediterranean, and from whence he proceeded along the Via

Appia to Rome. They show you the place where he landed, and we travelled along the same Via Appia. Here also we saw the ancient Amphitheatre (to which I have before alluded); it is in a very perfect state, larger than that at Pompeii, but smaller than the Colosseum. From thence the whole ride was one succession of objects of interest, temple after temple, the villa of Cicero, tombs, together with a volcanic mountain called the "Monte Nuovo," thrown up A.D. 1538, about a mile and a half in circumference and 440 feet above the level of the sea. Next, we came to the famous lake of Avernus, spoken of by Virgil in the 6th Book of the Æneid, from which he describes the descent to Hades, where Æneas went. It is also referred to in Homer's Odyssey. The scenery around it is now very beautiful, and the whole place strikingly picturesque, the Lake (still called by its ancient name) lying embosomed in cultivated slopes, so that A—— exclaimed at our first sight of it: "A jolly place, these infernal regions!" We had soon, however, reason to know that it more resembled the Poet's description than we imagined. For, bye and bye, we came to the real entrance, and the Cave of the Sybil. Here A—— and I got out, but the ladies remained in the carriage. We were provided with guides and torches, and entered a cavern on the banks of the Lake, through which we walked for a quarter of a mile, then a narrow passage branched off, just wide enough to admit one person. Here our principal guide left us, and we went on with two only and three torches. Presently we came to water, and were obliged to mount on their backs. They carried us through this water till we were alighted on a spot which was called "the Bath of the Sybil," where was an aperture in the rock, through which she was consulted and gave her responses; then we went on again in the same way through the water, till we came to the Palace of the Sybil, where there are some old remains of mosaic, and an Image of the Sybil. The whole place was as like as one can imagine to a descent to the infernal regions. After visiting the Baths of Nero, where the water rises to a temperature of 182, and which are used as vapour baths in rheumatic cases, we went to Baiæ, where we lunched. Of this place Horace says—

"*Nullus in orbe locus Baiis prælucet amœnis,*"

and a delightful place it certainly is, but marred since Horace's time by an ugly building or two;—thence to Misenum, where we visited the veritable Elysian Fields of the Ancients, now a rich vineyard—filled with ancient tombs. I forget to mention that we also visited Cumæ.

On our way back A—— and I got out and went up the volcanic mount of Solfatara, I on a donkey and A—— on foot. This mountain is always in action when Vesuvius is quiescent, and we saw the vapour and steam rushing out from an aperture, where there were internal noises like the boiling of water. From thence I had a very awkward ride over the rocks till we descended the mountain on the other side, but the scenery was the most beautiful of any I have seen in this lovely country, and I am glad the last impression was the best. In fact I am delighted with South Italy, and should be glad to spend a month there, provided it be not in Naples, which we both dislike much on account of the beggars, cheats, fleas, flies, and narrow dirty streets. The heat in the day is excessive, but altogether the climate and country suit me very well, and although I still have the pain in my back, it does not disable me.

Rome, Wednesday.—We have been finishing off some sights here to-day—the places where S. Paul lodged, S. Peter was crucified, on both which churches are built. To-morrow we reach Ancona, where we shall pass Friday, go to Bologna Saturday, and to Venice Monday. We shall stay there till towards the end of the week, and then to Milan.

Rome, May 8th.—I add a few lines to assure you I am getting better daily, this climate, I mean that of South Italy, suiting me wonderfully, although the heat is tremendous. Rome appears to much greater advantage after Naples, which, as regards the streets and people, is odious, but in respect of natural situation and surrounding country, magnificent—nothing yet has pleased me so much as South Italy. After Rome and Naples I do not seem to care much for what there is left to see. The Elysian Fields are well placed by the Ancients in South Italy, it contains some of the most charming spots on earth. We had the Duke of N—— and his tutor at our Table d'Hôte at Naples. I became acquainted with the latter before knowing who he was.

Bologna, 12th May.—The heat here to-day is so intense that it keeps everyone indoors, and I will, therefore, devote some of my leisure to writing a few lines in anticipation of the budget of news, which I expect to receive on our arrival at Venice to-morrow evening. In my letter from Rome on Wednesday I mentioned that we had finished off our sight-seeing there. This consisted in visiting the Basilica of Santa Croce, the floor of which is said to be formed of earth brought by S. Helena from Jerusalem; and the portion of the true Cross, which she brought from Jerusalem, was deposited here, and is the same as was exposed at S. Peter's on Good Friday; also the churches of S. Trinità de' Monti and S. Stefano Rotondo—also the church of S. Maria in the Via Lata, which occupies the spot where S. Paul lodged with the centurion. In the subterranean church beneath is a spring of water, which is said to have sprung up miraculously, to enable the Apostle to baptize his disciples—also the church of S. Pietro in Montorio. In the cloister of the adjoining monastery is a small circular temple, erected over the spot where S. Peter suffered martyrdom. The hole in which the cross was fixed is shown. We also visited the Ghetto—the place where the Jews in Rome are compelled to reside, being in one of the lowest and dirtiest parts. On Thursday morning we started from Rome to Ancona, having two of our Vesuvian party, Mrs. and Miss M——, for our travelling companions—also a French viscount and his lady, with whom I had a very agreeable conversation. They live at Nantes, and I feel inclined to call on them on my way home. The whole route from Rome to Ancona is full of beauty, particularly the latter part, where we cross the Apennines, which rise majestically on each side, the valleys being richly cultivated with vines and corn. We meant to have stayed a day at Ancona, but as I slept with my window open towards the sea, I was so dreadfully stung with mosquitoes (I believe) that I resolved to leave it the next morning, which we accordingly did, and went with Mrs. and Miss M—— to Ravenna. We had the King of Bavaria and his suite in the train, and I travelled in the same carriage with an Austrian count and his sister, on their way home from Egypt, where the latter had gone for her health, being consumptive—a very nice and interesting girl, who spoke English fluently. I mentioned in my last that we had the Duke of N—— at our Table d'Hôte at Naples, so that we have fallen in with all grades of society. With Ravenna I was very much pleased, it is rich in historical associations, and was selected by Lord Byron above all other places in Italy for his residence. We visited both the houses in which he lived, and where he composed many of his poems. It is also famous for containing the tomb of Dante, which we visited, though without paying the honour to it which Chateaubriand did, who knelt bareheaded at the door before he entered, or Alfieri, who prostrated himself before it. On Tuesday evening, we and the two ladies drove about two miles out of the city to see the famous church of S. Apollinare in Classe, which is a basilica, and said to contain a finer specimen of

Christian art than is to be found even in Rome; —thence to a large Pine Forest, whose praises have been celebrated by Dante, Bocaccio, Dryden, and Byron. It is very magnificent, and presents a vast succession of lovely avenues and glades. It was a favourite ride of Byron's over its turf. Next day being market day, we strolled through the market where all the country people had brought their commodities, and visited the cathedral with its beautiful baptistry and the magnificent basilica of San Vitale, built in the reign of Justinian in imitation of S. Sophia at Constantinople. This in my opinion comes nearest to S. Peter's of anything I have yet seen, and but for some wretched modern painting, would surpass it; indeed, considering the interest attached to its ancient mosaics, I am almost inclined to say it does surpass it. These are of the time of Justinian, and are as fresh and beautiful as when they were first placed there. We also went over the Academy of the Fine Arts. Ravenna is a quiet, clean, respectable old city, with good broad streets, and but little known to travellers. As a city it is in my opinion superior to Rome, that is, Modern Rome, and takes its place after Genoa. I was very much pleased with it—it was such a contrast to Naples and Rome. I forgot to say of Ancona that it was beautifully situated on a bay of the

Adriatic, but, like all sea ports, full of a low kind of population. A great part of our ride was along the coast. We and our two lady friends arrived at Bologna yesterday about 3.0 p.m. The ride was through a plain and richly-cultivated country called the Romagna. We immediately went to business, saw the church of S. Petronius, the largest in this place and built in the Italian Gothic style, but still unfinished—very handsome. On the floor is the celebrated meridian line of Cassini placed A.D. 1653;—thence to the church of S. Dominico, containing the tomb of the famous S. Dominic, the founder of the order of Preaching Friars—this is extremely beautiful; —also the tomb of Guido, the great painter;— thence to the church of S. Bartolomeo, where is a miracle-working picture of the Madonna. This was so enriched with presents of jewels, &c., that they, picture and all, were a few years ago stolen and taken to London, where the picture was afterwards found and brought back with great solemnity and rejoicing—the whole day being kept as a festival by the Bolognese. In the evening we took a drive to the church of S. Michele in Bosco, a little way out of the city, on an eminence which commands a most magnificent view of the city and the plain of the Romagna to an immense extent. This is much the best city we have yet seen in Italy, most of the streets having covered porticoes, which shelter from the sun and rain, and every thing bearing the appearance of plenty and respectability.

Sunday.—We attended service this morning at 11.0, at a room in the hotel, conducted by a clergyman, at which several were present. In the afternoon, notwithstanding the extreme heat, we drove out to the Campo Santo, or public cemetery, which is unrivalled by any in Europe and quite a sight for travellers, nothing could be more admirably contrived or managed. In the evening we took a drive with a Bolognese gentleman and his daughter, whom I had sat next to at the Table d'Hôte on that and the preceding day, and then asked them to name any pretty drive; they very politely offered to take us one, and a most beautiful one it was; we returned by moonlight and saw for the first time the swarm of sparkling fire-flies, having the appearance of a shower of fire as they danced about the corn field. They look like glowworms and at first I thought they were, but you soon see them dancing about the air. We have joined our Vesuvian party again here, very gentlemanly and pleasant people.

Monday.—We went to the top of a hill called the "Monte della Gardia," which commands a magnificent view from the Adriatic to the Alps and Apennines, with the rich plain of the Romagna spread out below, studded with cities, villages, churches, &c. On the top is the church of the Madonna de S. Lucca, so called from a miraculous picture of the Virgin attributed to S. Luke, which is kept there. The walk up the hill under a covered portico, of upwards of a mile, was tremendous and such as a short time ago I could never have accomplished. The portico, which extends about two miles from the city to the top of the hill, was built by the inhabitants for the purpose of a procession of the Madonna, which takes place once a year, and is one of their greatest public festivals. The walk is considered a pilgrimage, and such it really is, and we witnessed the adoration paid by the worshippers. The priest came and unlocked the door of the recess, the people all kneeling round, and exposed the picture—nothing could exceed the veneration paid to it. They took hold of a little velvet hanging below the picture, kissed it and pressed it to their foreheads. The picture was surrounded with jewels and precious stones that had been presented to it. We afterwards went over the Museum, Picture Gallery, and University Library. The Picture Gallery contains a famous one by Raphael, namely, Santa Cæcilia, of which I bought a photograph. On the whole we are much pleased with Bologna and are disappointed only in the *sausages*, which are served daily at the Table d'Hôte dinner, and are not so good as might be expected. I forgot to mention in my last, that at Baiæ we had a bottle of Horace's famous "Falernian," which still maintans its fine quality. For myself, I am quite another person. Italy has done wonders for me, and I begin to see now the absolute necessity there was for the change, for it has taken a long time to bring me round.

Venice, Tuesday.—We arrived here last night, leaving our friends Mrs. and Miss M—— at Ferrara on the way. I had a most delicious row in a gondola for about a mile from the railway station to the hotel, where we are very comfortable, and the row was a great treat after the noise and dust of the train. Here we have found many of our former friends, which is very agreeable. This morning I went to the post office and found a letter from W——, with instructions for my route home through Switzerland. I think of returning over the Simplon Pass from Milan and going from thence to Geneva, and making that my head quarters for some time, as there is a first-rate professor of the French language there from whom I want to take some lessons, as it worries me much not to be able to speak French. A—— had then better return, and I can work my way home at leisure. I hope any letters giving an account of our daily proceedings up to last Wednesday, when we left Rome, have been received. To-day we have been with Mr. and Mrs. K——, who were at our hotel at Rome and Naples, over S. Mark's Cathedral, and afterwards to the Ducal Palace, but I was so weary after my "pilgrimage" to S. Lucca at Bologna yesterday, that I came back soon after 3.0 for a nap. I am writing this before dinner. The Piazza dè San Marco and cathedral are very beautiful, and the views over the sea lovely. We also went to the Rialto, where Shylock complained that Antonio had so often "rated" him "about his monies and his usances." There is a bridge over one of the canals called the Rialto bridge, with shops on each side, and this is still one of the great thoroughfares of the place. It is very charming to have no noise of carriages and horses, and no dust. A—— found this morning that his leather bag had been cut open somewhere, and a pair of trousers abstracted. There are a dreadful set of rogues in Italy, from the brigands downwards. An English clergyman who had lately been to Naples said of it: "The city is a dunghill, and the inhabitants rogues and beggars." This is tolerably true. I am sorry to have disobeyed your orders in going to Naples, but I am sure I am none the worse for it, and it was a great treat, save the city itself and its inhabitants. We saw a curious thing at St. Mark's to-day. A large flock of pigeons have frequented it from time immemorial, which are fed at the expense of the government, and just before the clock strikes two they flock to the Piazza di San Marco to be fed, and are all assembled by the time the clock strikes. They are held in a sort of superstitious veneration by the people.

Wednesday.—We have been with Mr. and Mrs. K—— going about Venice in a gondola seeing churches. We shall leave this in three or four days for Milan, and proceed from thence to Como, and afterwards by a route W—— has sent me to Baveno, and cross the Simplon for Geneva. I am getting quite tired of roaming about and sight-seeing, and shall be very glad to rest on the banks of the lake of Geneva. A—— is very well and gets on with his Italian.

Milan, May 19th.—We arrived here last night, and I have to-day received your letter of the 16th. My object in writing at once is to say that I have altered my plans, and shall go from Lake Como to Paris and not to Geneva, and make the former my head quarters, where A—— will leave me for England. Perhaps you and M——, or one of you, might like to join me there to see the Exhibition, but I will write again. I want to have some lessons in French when at Paris, as the not being able to converse in it has worried me exceedingly. Afterwards, I thought of working my way quietly home through Brittany. I suppose I shall reach Paris within a fortnight from this time.

I was greatly delighted with Venice, saw all the churches and picture galleries, the Doge's Palace and the Bridge of Sighs, with mention of which Lord Byron begins his 4th canto of Childe Harold. We also rowed about a good deal, and went to Murano, but not to Torcello—in fact, I wanted to spend yesterday and to-day longer in Venice, but A—— seemed to wish to get away. One evening we spent with a party in the Piazzo di S. Marco, which is the general rendezvous for all the respectable inhabitants on an evening—where they stroll or sit and drink coffee, and chat. The piazza itself is most beautiful, surpassing any other place of the kind I have seen, and these social gatherings make the people appear like one large family. We had one long row on the Lagoon by moonlight, which was most lovely. This "Queen of the Adriatic" is certainly also the Queen of Cities. We are also much pleased with Milan. After attending the English church this morning, we went with Mr. and Mrs. K—— (whom we found here) to the cathedral;—here we were struck with amazement indeed,—in both exterior and interior it surpasses S. Peter's, and of course every other cathedral or church, out and out. Besides, being Gothic and having splendid painted windows, it is more in accordance with our English ideas. To-morrow we intend to go over it fully, but a day might be well employed upon it. A—— remarked that it was worth the whole journey to Milan to see it. We have since been with Mr. K—— to the public gardens, where all the city stroll out on Sunday afternoons. All social life on the Continent seems to be public—so different from ours! On Tuesday or Wednesday we shall leave for Lake Como, and from thence probably over the Simplon to Lucerne and Paris. I shall be very sorry to turn my back on Italy. Read what Lord Byron says of it in canto IV. of Childe Harold, stanzas 25 and 26. I quite respond to it. The dinner bell rings—Good-bye.

Lugano, May 27th.—I have half an hour to spare before leaving this place which I will devote to writing this letter. My last letter was, I believe, despatched from Milan yesterday week, that is, on Sunday the 19th. We enjoyed Milan very much—it is decidedly the best city in Italy as a city, Naples and Venice of course having the advantage of situation. There are beautiful public gardens and drives near, where the whole city seem to assemble on Sunday afternoons and evenings, which we visited with the K——s, whom we found here. On Monday we went in company with them over Milan Cathedral, of which (I believe) I expressed my opinion in my last, that it surpassed my expectations beyond anything I had seen since I left England. S. Peter's, although much larger, is not to be compared with it externally or internally for grandeur, beauty, or religious impressiveness. It is Gothic, and contains some splendid painted glass—has 386 gurgoyles, all different—8000 carved flowers, all different—146 pinnacles, each containing twenty-five statues, all different. I shall never forget the impression of the first entrance into it, for the light through the painted windows being dim, the interior gradually opens to the eye, as it becomes accustomed to the gloom from the glare outside, and the splendid proportions and beautiful work of the cathedral develope themselves. Moreover, all is solid white marble. S. Carlo Borromeo, who was one of the principal benefactors to Milan, and did a great part towards the restoration of the cathedral, lies interred there in a magnificent silver shrine. I attended high mass on Monday and Tuesday mornings, when the organ was played, and (if I mistake not) S. Augustine says in his "Confessions," that the music of the divine services he heard in Milan Cathedral had a great effect in producing his conversion, and he particularly describes the emotions he felt under it. S. Ambrose was then the bishop, and by him S. Augustine was afterwards baptized. The Ambrosian Rite has still been preserved in Milan, and is said to be the only one in the West which has been spared by the Roman Church, the clergy and people being very jealous of it, and having resisted every attempt to have the Roman Liturgy forced upon them. I observed that it differed much from the Roman, and that there was no prostration or bell-ringing at the elevation of the host. I bought a copy of the Ordinary of the Mass, to compare it with the Roman when I get home. We afterwards visited several churches and public places, the principal of which was the basilica of S. Ambrozio, founded by S. Ambrose, and dedicated by him to the martyrs SS. Gervasius and Protasius. Here are the panels of the door which S. Ambrose closed against the Emperor Theodosius. In the crypt under the altar are the tombs of S. Ambrose and SS. Gervasius and Protasius. The next thing particularly worth mentioning was the famous painting of Leonardo da Vinci's "Last Supper," said to have been the finest in the world, but now, alas! sadly disfigured by the hand of Time, owing to the peculiar process that was used in forming the ground-work of the painting, which is a frescoe on the walls of the refectory of an old convent. The expression of our Saviour's face, which was the most remarkable part of the painting, is that which has least suffered from the decay. The next day (Tuesday) we went up part of the Tower or Campanile of the Cathedral, where we had a very fine view of its exterior and of the city and adjoining country, and went over the sculp-. tures and pictures in the Brera, a large public palace,—and afterwards the Bibliotheca Ambrosiana, which contains some valuable MSS. and autographs of eminent persons, including S. Philip de Neri, S. Francis de Sales, and S. Carlo Borromeo. This day we found some of our old Naples friends, whom we had also met at Bologna and Venice, and they offered us places in a box at the opera, which we accepted. This was the first theatre I had attended since I left England, the performance was very good, but both the words and the plot being quite unintelligible to me, I got weary and left before it was finished. The next morning (Wednesday) we started for Lake Como, stopping at Monza on the way, in order to see the famous Iron Crown of Lombardy. The origin of it is lost in remote antiquity, but the traditions of Monza say that it was given by Gregory the Great to Queen Theodolinda, who seems to have been as great a monarch in Lombardy as Elizabeth in England. Thirty-five Kings of Lombardy have been crowned with it in the Cathedral of Monza, Charles V. being the last of the later Emperors that were crowned with it until Napoleon I., anxious to connect his dignity with the recollections of the past, placed it with his own hands upon his head, disdaining to receive it from the bishop. It has since been used at the coronation of the two last Emperors of Austria. The crown itself is a fillet of gold studded with jewels, but having inside it a rim of iron, said to have been hammered out from one of nails used at the Crucifixion. Hence it is called "*Il sacro Chiodo.*" It is safely guarded in an iron closet let into the wall of the cathedral, and a good deal of ceremony was used before we could see it. First, we had to show our passports, and then wait a quarter of an hour, after which came two priests in their robes, a thurifer also robed, and another man with planks and steps and red hangings. With these he formed a sort of platform under the iron closet, on which he hung the drapery and there fixed the steps. Three massive locks were then turned and curtains drawn aside, the two priests knelt, and the thurifer swung his censer with the burning incense, and the Iron Crown was let down for us to examine, and with the same ceremony put back again. At the same time was shown to us a glass cross, set in a gold frame and containing some pieces of the True Cross—of the Sponge—of the Holy Sepulchre—of the Reed held by Christ—one of the Thorns of the Crown—and some Stones of the Pillar to which He was bound. During the interval of our waiting for the exhibition of the Iron Crown, we were shown the curiosities of the sacristy, consisting chiefly of things that had belonged to the famous Queen Theodolinda, such as her crown, fan, comb, cup, &c., but the most interesting of all was the list of relics sent by Gregory the Great to her, written on papyrus and said to contain his autograph. The celebrated Antiquary Maffei calls this "the King of Papyri." We then filled up our time before the train arrived, by taking a delightful drive through the park belonging the Royal Palace. The train took us to the shore of Lake Como, where we embarked on the steam-boat and had a most delightful passage up the Lake to Bellagio. The name of this lake has been familiar to me from boyhood as having been the place of residence of the unfortunate Queen Caroline at the Villa d'Este, which I saw from the steam-boat. This exquisite lake quite equalled all I had heard of it, which, in truth, was that it was "the Lake of Europe." We found Bellagio so full that we were not able to get accommodation, except at a third-rate hotel, although we had written to secure rooms. Here we fell in again with some of our former friends.

Thursday.—The K——s called and took us a delightful walk through the gardens and grounds of the Villa Serbelloni, from whence there are splendid views of the Lakes Como and Lecco and of the surrounding mountains. In the afternoon it blew a hurricane with thunder and lightning, and the lake was tossed like the sea. The next day (Friday) I walked again through the grounds of the Villa Serbelloni, and in the afternoon we left the place with the K——s and a clergyman and his wife and niece named F——, and crossed over the lake to Cadinabbia, hoping to find the C——s, but they had left for the Simplon Pass. With this place and the beautiful grounds of the Villa Carlotta I was much delighted, and think it far superior to Bellagio, although that is the most frequented place. The afternoon and evening were brilliant, and the setting sun bathed the upper half of the mountains round the lake with a ruby red. It was one of the loveliest sights you can conceive. The next morning (Saturday,) the K——s, F——s, and ourselves took a boat to Menaggio, and from thence an omnibus by ourselves to Porlezza, from whence we had a delightful passage by steam-boat down the Lake of Lugano to this place. Although the lake is not quite so picturesque as that of Como, I like the hotel and town better than any of the places on Lake Como, and could spend a few weeks here with great pleasure, and there are numerous walks about. Yesterday (Sunday) we attended divine service twice in a small building excellently fitted up as a church, the service being performed admirably by the Rev. Mr. C——, sent by the S. P. G., under the authority of the Bishop of London. I sat next him at dinner at the Table d'Hôte, and at breakfast next morning I had a very interesting conversation with him. There is a cathedral and several churches here, some of which I visited yesterday.

Hospenthal, Switzerland, May 29, 10.0 p.m.—I must resume my pen here, where we arrived about 8.0 this evening, Mr. and Mrs. K—— and ourselves took a private carriage from Lugano, Monday morning, for Luino on the Lake Maggiore, and thence by steam-boat down the lake to Stresa. It rained nearly all the way on the lake, so that we did not see much. The next morning was very fine, and the K——s

and ourselves took a boat to the Borromean
Islands of Isola Bella and Isola Madre, which
are celebrated for their beauty. I was greatly
pleased with Stresa, but on the whole should
prefer staying at Lugano to any other place on
the Italian Lakes. After a great deal of deliberation and consultation we determined with
the K——s to cross the Alps by the S. Gothard
Pass in a private carriage by ourselves, and
made the contract before we left Lugano. So
we quitted Stresa on Tuesday morning by
steam-boat for Magadino. The day was beautiful, and we had a most delightful passage up
the Lake Maggiore, which compensated for all
we had lost the day before. On the whole I
prefer this lake to either of the others—it has
more expanse and variety of scenery, though
not such beautiful points as Como. From
Magadino the K——s and we took a private
carriage to Bellinzona where we slept, and
started at 6.0 this morning for this place on our
way to Lake Lucerne. I cannot describe the
splendour of the scenery we have witnessed
to-day—first, for several hours through the Swiss
valleys between the mountains on our way to
the S. Gothard Pass, and then the Pass itself.
It is admitted to be the most terrific as well
as the most magnificent of all the Passes, and
I would not have missed it on any account.

To find oneself on the summit of the Alps in the midst of a world of snow, with the many crests of the gigantic range all around you, and stretching as far as the eye could reach, gave a feeling which no language can convey. The waterfalls all through the journey were magnificent, as was also the ascent up the Pass. The day was everything one could wish—scarce a cloud to be seen, and the rays of the setting sun on the snow-clad mountain-peaks gave great additional effect to the scene. We shall finish our descent to-morrow, and make for Flüelen, there embark on steamer for Lucerne, or rather for the Rigi mountain, which I mean to go up to-morrow evening, if possible, to take advantage of this fine weather for seeing the sun rise. I feel the mountain air to-day has done me so much good, and given me such elasticity of spirits, that I am inclined to change my plans again and stop at Lucerne. I have had a heavy day's work, and shall have another to-morrow—so must say good-night.

Lucerne, May 31st.—I hope that ere the receipt of this you will have had my letter posted at Hospenthal yesterday, in which I promised to write again from hence. Yesterday (Ascension Day) I joined a procession that passed the hotel between 7.0 and 8.0 a.m., and followed them to the church. A priest met them at the entrance, where they had a short out-of-door service, consisting of some antiphonal chanting, and prayers. Nothing could be more simple. The "Amens" to the prayers were beautiful, and different from any I had heard before—three notes to the first syllable and one to the last—men, women, and children, each assembling in separate bodies. A part of the first chapter of S. John's Gospel was read, and at the words "And the Word was made Flesh" (in Latin) they all knelt and rose again. After this little service was over, they went inside the church, which was soon filled to overflowing—men, women, and children still apart, and high mass was celebrated in full choral service with the organ and village choir. The simple and earnest devotion of the people was beautiful—all consisting of poor Alpine villagers, but as respectable in appearance as any village congregation in England on a Sunday. The singing also was very good. After the mass was over, a priest walked down the church and sprinkled all the congregation on both sides (including myself) with holy water. I observed that the day was kept very religiously all through our journey yesterday, as we saw the country people either going in or out of the churches, or passed them on the road with their books on their way from them—a great contrast indeed to the mode in which the day is observed in the villages in England! The wild magnificence of the scenery of the Mountain Pass yesterday from Hospenthal is far beyond description—there is one part called "The Devil's Bridge," which is very celebrated for its grandeur, and excursions are often made from hence to Hospenthal for the purpose of seeing the scenery. Besides the towering and snow-clad Alps, it consists of foaming cataracts, leaping waterfalls, and stupendous cliffs—interspersed here and there with pretty little Swiss villages in the green valleys; the road following by continual zigzags the course of the river Reuss the whole way—in fact we were for more than twenty miles continually descending, besides nine miles from the summit to Hospenthal the day before. The general impression it makes is that of stern grandeur and magnificence, just the opposite to the luxuriant garden of Italy. And yet I could not leave Italy without many a sigh, for she has satisfied to the full my every capacity of enjoyment, classical, historical, and archæological or ecclesiastical; she has that which can satisfy the tastes for all and each—and having myself a little turn for them all, she has made me brim-full of delight. I know not whether I shall ever see her face again—but certainly I shall not until I can converse with her in her own magnificent language. Hers is the land of loveliness—Switzerland of grandeur. The two therefore cannot be compared. Lord Byron, I think somewhere in "Childe Harold," having visited both, gives his preference to the former—and certainly (as I remarked) it contains more abundant food for all variety of tastes—for the Apennines are not without grandeur, any more than the Swiss Alpine villages are without loveliness. I did not mention yesterday the luxuriance of the gardens in the villas on the Italian lakes—magnolias growing like great trees—and camellias and azaleas large shrubs—besides splendid rhododendrons and wild cactuses. Our voyage up the Lake of Lucerne yesterday from Flüelen was very beautiful, and I think on the whole this lake excels the Italian ones, as it combines most of their beauties with a greater expanse. The part near Flüelen is like Lake Como, other parts like Lake Maggiore. Lucerne also is beautifully situate on its shores. We are with the K——s at the Swiss hotel facing the lake, which is bounded on the opposite side by the snowy Alps, having the Rigi at one end of the range and Mount Pilatus on the other, but everything pales after the splendid scenery of the last two days. The weather is intensely hot and the sky cloudless, and there was a fine sun-set yesterday, the rays of which are thrown on the mountains opposite. I forgot to say that we left Hospenthal yesterday about 9.0 a.m., and reached Flüelen on the bank of this lake about 2.0 p.m. in time for the steamer, and reached Lucerne about 5.0 p.m. I felt a good deal fatigued after yesterday's journey and my back is painful, but I intend going up the Rigi, if possible, to-day, and returning tomorrow after seeing sun-set and sun-rise. On Monday we propose going to Interlaken and reaching Paris on the following Monday or Tuesday in Whitsun-week. Mde. Taylor says she can take us in. A—— will leave me at Paris, and I propose following him slowly home, first taking some lessons in French. Let me find a letter when I reach Mde. Taylor's (94, Champs Elyseés), saying what you think of you and M——, or one of you, coming to the Exhibition. I do not delay writing, as you might be anxious to know that we got safely through the Pass, for without steady horses and driver it is very full of danger.

Berne, June 7th.—I hope my letter from Lucerne of last week has been received. I believe that was posted on Friday. On that day I fully meant to have ascended the Rigi, but the heat was intense, and the K——s ruled not to go, the weather also looked very threatening, indeed in the evening we had a tremendous thunder storm—so we merely strolled about and went to see Thorwaldsen's lions carved out of the rock, in memory of the Swiss Guards who fell in defending Louis XVI;—also the museum of stuffed Alpine animals, and a very good diorama of the Rigi and Mount Pilatus as seen at sun-set and sun-rise, so that I have seen both second-hand, as it were. The next day (Saturday) was too hot for anything, so I got up a party of upwards of twenty from the hotel to hear the cathedral organ played for an hour. Both organ and organist are very famous; we were charged a franc each, and the performance was admirable—particularly the imitation of the human voice and the thunder storm. In the evening we took a very pretty walk to a place called the Linden, overlooking the Lake, where we had a charming view of the Lake and mountain scenery on one side, and an extensive Swiss landscape on the other. On Sunday we went to the English church twice, and took a long walk in the evening, which was rather too much for me, and I have suffered in my back ever since. By "we" I mean Mr. K——, A——, and myself. We fell in, as usual, with former travelling acquaintances at Lucerne, which helped to pass away the time agreeably, otherwise I should have found it extremely dull, for I was very much vexed at missing the Rigi, having gone to Lucerne almost for the purpose. Perhaps it was as well I did not, for I was a good deal fatigued with my journey over the S. Gothard Pass, and my back ached much all Friday. By the way, I forgot to mention in my last that on our road from the Pass to Flüelen we went through the land of Tell, his birthplace, and the spot where he stood when he took the aim at the apple on his son's head, his statue being erected at the place. I was glad to get away from Lucerne, and started at 9.0 a.m. Monday morning with the K——s by steamer, and had a delightful passage down the Lake to Alpnach, where we took a private carriage for Interlaken. We had a pleasant ride over the Brünig Pass till we had passed Brienz, when the rain began to fall and continued till we reached Interlaken. I was unprepared to find it so much of a fashionable sort of watering place, and it reminded me of Malvern. As we did not intend staying beyond three days, we put up at the Victoria. The next day (Tuesday) poured with rain, so A—— and myself went by steamer to Giessbach, where we landed, and I got into a *chaise à porteur* to mount the hill for the hotel, getting out every now and then to have a better view of the Fall, which is magnificent, and particularly at this season of the year, when the quantity of water is great. We dined at the hotel, and returned by steamer in the evening. By Wednesday morning the weather had cleared up, so the K———'s and ourselves started in a carriage for Grindelwald, where we visited the Lower Glacier. I shall not dwell on this, as you have already seen it all. I was carried in a *chaise à porteur* to the glacier, when I got out and went with the others to the end of the tunnel of ice which had been cut into the glacier. The whole is very wonderful and interesting. The day was beautiful and clear after the rain, so we had splendid views of the mountains above the glacier. We drove to Lauterbrunnen, having magnificent views of the Jungfrau and Silberhorn Mountains on the way—indeed the latter part of the drive from where the road turns off to Grindelwald was extremely picturesque. On our arrival at Lauterbrunnen the K———s determined on returning to Interlaken, but as I had been disappointed of the Rigi, and had been told that the Wengen Alp was not passable, except by wading through snow, I determined to ascend the Mürren with A———, so I hired a horse and mounted for the night. It was a magnificent sun-set, and its rosy hues were thrown on the mountain tops as we ascended, adding greatly to the splendour of the scene. Before retiring to rest I enjoyed a beautiful moonlight view from the balcony of the hotel; the soft rays of a quarter moon thrown on the snowy heights gave them an exquisite silvery aspect and added to the intensity of the gloom cast by the shadow of the mountains on the opposite side of the gorge, while the hollow murmurings of the stream at the bottom of the gulf below gave a living character to this most picturesque scene. The next morning I rose at 4.0 a.m. and went out to the balcony. The sky was cloudless, and the scenes of yesterday were only surpassed by that of this morning, as I sat alone in the balcony for an hour and a half, gazing in silent admiration. One snowy peak after another was touched with the living fire of the sun's rays, while other mountains were gradually becoming bathed in light—and the snow sparkled like diamonds in beautiful contrast to the soft placid appearance which it wore under the moonbeam the night before. I am particularly fortunate in one respect in travelling through Switzerland at this time, for the winter having been unusually severe and the spring late, there is more than the ordinary quantity of snow on the mountains at this season, and every day now lessens it. A—— rose at the same time as myself and walked to the hill above, but did not seem so struck with the beauty of the scene as myself—perhaps because he was walking and could not fix that steady gaze on it which I did. After breakfast we and another party descended—I on foot very slowly, and with the help of an arm the greater part of the way. We saw your name and that of the rest of your party in the traveller's book here and at Grindelwald. The impression which the path has left on my mind is not unmixed with terror at the sight of that monster Jungfrau staring you full in the face from head to foot, and I believe in no part of Switzerland is there so perfect a view of a mountain from top to bottom to be seen. We drove back to Interlaken after visiting the Staubbach Fall, the party we met giving us a seat in their carriage, and embarked on the steamer for this place at 5.0 p.m. Interlaken being so hot and close, I was not sorry to leave it. I passed the Hôtel de Beau Site, and saw there was a splendid mountain view from it. We had a delightful sail up the lake of Thun, and the mountain scenery from it is the best I have yet seen for a distant view. We are now about to start to see this town (Berne) and then go by rail to Dijon, where we shall sleep to-night and reach Paris to-morrow (Saturday) night.

12.30.—I am just returned from a drive to see "the lions" and the bears. Of the former there are but few, the chief are the cathedral, a melancholy mixture of a Methodist chapel and a church, the museum of stuffed animals, and some fine views of the city and country backed by the Bernese Oberland. The latter consist of four veritable live animals of that name, kept in a public open space—the town (they say) deriving its name from these creatures. I am now taking my leave of Switzerland, as I have done from Italy. The most vivid impression she has left upon me is (as usual) the *first*, that is, the sight from the summit of the S. Gothard Pass. I was there under peculiarly advantageous circumstances. The vast accumulation of snow from the hard winter and long spring gave the whole plateau the appearance of one vast region of snow, broken only by the wild mountain-peaks in every direction as far as the eye could reach. Besides, we had come to it along a road in many places just wide enough to take the carriage wheels, and cut through walls of snow twenty or thirty feet high. The Pass had only been opened the week before, and since then it had been closed up with snow, so that I had determined not to come by it until the Maitre d'Hôtel at Lugano assured me it was reopened. Then the exhilarating effect of the air was most wonderful, for we were 6,800 feet above the level of the sea, the Rigi being 5,900, and

Symondshall Down 800, and yet the difference in the feeling which the latter gives of lightness and buoyancy is very perceptible. The sight was so strange and wonderful that I shall never lose its effect—all mountaineers say it is the invigorating feeling of the air that enables them to perform their feats. Then followed, the next day, that most splendid route through one of the wildest gorges in Switzerland, so celebrated that it forms of itself one of the excursions for tourists to see it. Although therefore my acquaintance with Switzerland has been much shorter than that with Italy, I have fallen in love with her too, notwithstanding her beauties are of a different kind from my charming Italy. It is now I know not how long since I have heard from any of you, more than three weeks, I think. I hope when I get to Paris the news will be all good.

(a) Paris, June 21st.—I want to get out of this hot place as soon as possible, so have proposed that E—— and I start for Geneva Sunday night. We shall stay at Geneva on Monday, and then go on to Chamounix, making that our head quarters. It seems a pity to lose the chance when I am half way there, and I think the mountain air will do me great good. I and

---

(a) The letters written during a fortnight's sojourn in Paris at the time of the Exhibition are missing.

my two nieces have been at the Louvre all the morning, but I long to get away from this place. The heat is overpowering.

Frohburg, near Olten, June 28th.—You will be surprised to receive a letter from me here— an out-of-the-world little hotel on the Jura mountains, remarkable for its pure air and commanding very picturesque scenery. I was induced to come here instead of the Rigi, from accounts I had of it in my travels, but shall leave again to-morrow morning for Geneva, still retaining my intention of returning to England with E—— the beginning of the following week. We left Paris on Monday morning and arrived at Strasbourg the same evening, and had a turn in the public promenade in the middle of the city late in the evening, while the band was playing. Next morning, we visited the cathedral and church of S. Thomas. The exterior of the former is very fine, but the interior not equal to our English cathedrals. At twelve o'clock I went again to hear the wonderful clock strike. This clock is a celebrated piece of mechanism, showing not only the hours of the day, but the motion of the sun, moon, and stars. At twelve o'clock daily the twelve Apostles come out in succession, each making obeisance to our Lord as they pass Him standing in the centre, and proclaim noon by striking a blow with a hammer on a bell. Then a cock (which is a piece of clock-work) claps his wings, stretches his neck, and gives a crow with all the importance and intonation of the natural bird. So perfect is this, that a clergyman with whom I travelled would not believe but that the "crow" was made by some human being concealed for the purpose. A crowd was assembled in the cathedral to witness the sight. We saw several storks in the city; they build their nests on the tops of the chimneys. We afterwards started for Basle, and next day (Wednesday) visited the cathedral and the tombs and monuments of Erasmus, Œcolampadius, and others of the Reformers;— thence to the museum and picture gallery, the latter containing some good paintings, particularly those by Holbein who lived at Basle. The original "Dance of Death" was painted on the walls of the cathedral, and some remains of it are still left. The organ was being played and it is a very fine one. In the chapter house was held the Council of Basle in the 15th century. There are some very interesting original portraits by Holbein in the museum, particularly one of Edward VI. and of Sir Thomas More and his family—two of Erasmus, one when alive and another after his death—also of Luther and his wife and of Melancthon by

Cranach. We also saw the book of Erasmus in which humorous marginal illustrations had been made by the pen of Holbein, which so amused Erasmus that it threw him into a violent fit of laughter, causing an abscess from which he was suffering to burst, and so cured him of his illness. We also visited the house where he lodged. After that we started for Zurich on our way to the Rigi, and slept at Zurich Wednesday night. It is a very nice place, but not equal to Lucerne. Instead of going up the Rigi, however, I changed my plans and came here, where we slept last night. We saw a splendid sun-set from Zurich, the rays falling on the Alps of the Bernese Oberland, and bringing them out in full grandeur. We came here yesterday in a violent storm of thunder and lightning, but to-day it is bright and clear and the views magnificent. We hope to reach Geneva to-morrow evening, and go on Monday to Chamounix, and remain there till Saturday, then return to Geneva, and on the following Monday return to Paris and arrive in London on Wednesday, which is the last day of E——'s return ticket. I am heartily tired of this roaming life, and there are no associations in this country to interest one as in Italy, and relieve the fatigue of railway travelling. I have the greatest aversion also to the German language, which is like a perpetual saw to my brain. At Geneva I shall escape it. I could make my way very fairly well in French, and should not mind travelling alone where that language is spoken, but shall nevertheless return. All in this hotel jabber away in German, which is partly the reason of my leaving it. A letter would find me at Chamounix on or before Friday next.

Chamounix, July 3rd.—We arrived here from Geneva on Monday evening, and I was disappointed at not finding any letters, the last I received being at Paris last Sunday week. My last to you was from Frohburg, and to T—— *(a)* from Geneva. I was much pleased with the former place, but the company were nearly all German whose language I nauseated; the situation, however, was beautiful and the air delicious. On our route to Geneva, on Saturday, we had a splendid view of the Savoy range of Alps from the train, and Mont Blanc came out in her full white robe tinged with the pink of the setting sun in all her greatness—not a cloud to be seen. We spent Sunday in Geneva and attended the English church twice. My back was bad and I made an effort to get to the cathedral in the afternoon but could not accomplish it. There is very little attractive in

---

(a) This letter is missing.

Geneva, the lake and houses are fine, but there are no names connected with it except Calvin, Rousseau, and Voltaire (whose residence called "Fernie," was about two miles off). Rousseau's statue is in the middle of the city—why they should have preferred him to Calvin, they best know. I was delighted to fall in at the Table d'Hôte with a Russian family, consisting of a count, his wife, and children, who had been five times in Italy, and the countess was so enthusiastic about it that she would not allow a word to be said against any of the inhabitants, or that the Neapolitans were worse than the rest of the world. I did not see them again afterwards as we left early next morning, but I should have liked much to have had some more conversation with them. They spoke capital English. On our way to Geneva we passed through Freybourg and Lausanne, two very fine towns, and the latter having splendid mountain scenery at the head of the Lake of Geneva. There was a very pretty scene near Berne as we passed along,—a sort of festival with wrestling games going on in the fields and a number of flags and a great concourse of people. On our way from Geneva here we took part of a carriage with a very nice couple, a gentleman and lady just returned from visiting Egypt and the whole of Palestine and Italy. I pumped him hard about Jerusalem and the Holy Land. He was at Jerusalem at Easter, last year, and at Rome at the same festival, this year. His tastes exactly coincided with my own about Italy and all the objects of interest, particularly Milan Cathedral. We had a magnificent view of Mont Blanc and all the range, as we approached Chamounix, the sky being cloudless. Yesterday we went on mules a two hours' ride to Montanvert, to have the best view of the famous glacier called the "Mer de Glace." It was a very grand and wondrous sight. It began to rain just as we reached the little inn, and continued to do so nearly all the day—nevertheless E—— and a large party from the inn crossed the glacier and got home through the Chapeau and the Mauvais Pas. I had neither umbrella nor great coat and only my straw hat, and after waiting several hours for the rain to cease, I at last took a bed for the night, but the weather clearing I changed my plans and came down. E—— got thoroughly soaked and lost the view—the former she disregarded but the latter was no small disappointment to her. My guide was one of the seven who went to find the body of poor Mr. Young last year. I have this morning had a long conversation with another of them, who produced to me his medal which the Emperor of the French gave to each of them for their conduct on that occasion. They were seen to fall by a gentleman, through a telescope from one of the hotels. To-morrow, if the weather permit, we propose going to the Flegère and the Grotto of Ice at the source of the Arveron, and returning to Geneva on Saturday, so as to reach London on Wednesday. Yesterday, the first party this season started from hence for the summit of Mont Blanc, we went very near them on our way to the Mer de Glace. This day, we have been much interested in watching them through a capital telescope at the hotel. They have not gone far yet and the rain yesterday must have stopt them. I have changed my bed-room to-day for one which looks direct on Mont Blanc, so that I hope to see the sun rise on it to-morrow morning. This place is too hot for me, and but for the sights I should not stay here. It is too much shut in by the mountains, although about 3,000 feet above the level of the sea. The summit of Mont Blanc is 15,784 feet, the highest point in Europe—it is just above Chamounix, which is in fact situate on the range. I am quite sure that a *dry, fresh air* is what suits me, such as that in Rome and Naples, which had a most wonderful effect on me. The air there is quite free from vapour, which makes the atmosphere look so peculiarly clear, as though we were moving in a vacuum. I attribute it to the effect of the dry air from Africa on one side, and from the Apennines and the Campagna on the other, notwithstanding its being surrounded by the sea.

Paris, July 8th. — We left Chamounix on Saturday morning at 7.0, and travelled without stopping the twenty-four hours, till we arrived here at the same hour yesterday morning. As it is expensive stopping here, we propose leaving to-morrow morning for London and arriving at Ewell to-morrow evening. I shall want three or four days in town, and hope to see you once more towards the end of the week. We were much interested at Chamounix by the party who ascended Mont Blanc, the first since the fatal accident to Capt. Arkwright, his porters, and guide last year,—and it being the first since the winter season, and no experience of the effect and operation of the winter's snow, some apprehensions were felt. I watched them through an excellent telescope up and down. The guns in the village fired when they reached the summit, and when they returned,—and a concourse of people, including myself, went to meet them. Next morning I went to their hotel and had some chat with them—they were very gentlemanly men.

Old England again!
July 10.

We arrived at Ewell safe, soon after 10.0 p.m. yesterday, having had a very good passage. I took the chloroform and lay down on my back as soon as I got into the cabin, and although rather uncomfortable, was not ill. The sea was smooth. We saw the review in Paris by the Sultan and Emperor on Monday —40,000 troops.

I have called at Dr. Gull's to-day, and got an appointment for Friday at 9.0 a.m., the earliest I could get, and purpose leaving this the same afternoon, and reaching Dursley by the train which arrives at 9.10 p.m.

I shall be very glad to be with you all once more.

APPENDIX.
—oo—

In the foregoing Letters allusion is made to my having seen in the Laurentian Library at Florence an original copy of the Decree of the Council of Florence. This copy is in two parts, Greek and Latin, written side by side on the same vellum. To the Greek are attached the autograph signatures of the Emperor John Palæologus, the Patriarchal Vicars, Bishops, and other representatives of the Eastern Church, and to the Latin those of Pope Eugenius IV., and the Cardinals, Bishops, and other representatives of the Western Church.

This Council (which was held in the 15th Century) was considered to be Œcumenical, and an important question has arisen whether or not it concedes to the Pope that unlimited authority, which he claims, of governing the whole Church. The Greek version of the Decree admits a restricted authority only, as prescribed by the Acts of Œcumenical Councils, and the Holy Canons; while the Latin Version, according to some readings, exactly agrees with the Greek, but according to others is so worded as to yield to the Pope all the privileges which he claims. The reader will see the whole subject discussed in an Article signed "Edmund S. Ffoulkes" in the "Union Review" for March, 1866. When I saw the original Decree in the Library at Florence, I attempted to hold some conversation in Latin with the Assistant Librarian there on the point in dispute relative to the wording of the Latin Version, and obtained his permission to correspond with him on the subject. Accordingly I addressed him from Rome a letter, of which the following is a copy :—

"Hôtel de la Pension Anglaise,
Via Condotti, Romæ,
19 April. 1867.

Vir Reverende,

Colloquium nostrum die quinto Aprilis in Bibliothecâ de "San Lorenzo" habitum revocare liceat. MS. acta Concilii Florentini tractabamus, et in animo est ut certior factus sim de verbis Græcè redditis "καθ' ὃν τρόπον * * * * διαλαμβάνεται." Sed haud scio an sint Latinè reddita "*quemadmodum* ETIAM * * * * *continetur*," an rectins "*quemadmodum* ET *in actis Œcumenicorum Conciliorum, et in sacris canonibus constituitur*."—In Angliâ de his verbis sæpe agitur, et mihi valde interest ipsissima verba MSti cognoscere, cujus te testem citare volo. Secundum verbum tuum in charitate tuâ epistolam mittas mihi hic moranti infra sex dies.

Reverende Vir,
Tui observantissimus,
J. V."

Revdo. Ab. Dott. Niciola Anziani,
Adjutori in Bibliothecâ Laurentianâ,
Florence.

To this letter I received the following answer :—

"Florentiæ.

Præclare Vir,

Tuis litteris celerius respondissem, si mihi tempestive advectæ essent : sed cum hodie solum mihi redditæ sint, nollem me nomine negligentiæ tibi suspectum esse, si hodie tantummodo tibi respondeam. Pergratum mihi fecisti præbendo locum ex Decreto Concilii Florentini, ex quo præsertim in tuâ patriâ multæ exortæ sunt contentiones circa textum Græcum et fidem interpretationis Latinæ, quæque me prorsus latuerant, ita ut et tuam obstupeam doctrinam, et meæ me pudeat ignorantiæ. En, textum Græcum tibi describo et Lat. interpret. sicuti extant in charta originali apud nos servatâ.

* * * * καθ' ὃν τρόπον καὶ ἐν τοῖς πρακτικοῖς τῶν οἰκουμενικῶν συνόδων, καὶ τοῖς ἱεροῖς κανόσι διαλαμβάνεται * * * * *(in edit. καὶ ἐν τοῖς ἱεροῖσ)*

* * * * *quemadmodum etiam in gestis Œcumenicorum Conciliorum et in sacris Canonibus continetur.*

Si textus Græcus vel ne Latino respondeat adamussim, nec judicare auserim, quippe qui doctrinæ expers et autoritatis: sed tantum mihi dicere liceat, si veniam mihi concedis pro tuâ humanitate, quod versio non curat reddere verbum verbo,—nam hoc locutionem efficere potuisset pene barbaram ac prope omni luciditate detracta,—sed ita efficta, ut integer præsertim existat sensus, et verborum fides tenacior servetur, *si possit.* Quapropter si judicium instituatur de fide verborum, versio infidelis; si de sensu et perspicuitate, optima ac prorsus respondens.—Vale.

Tuus famulus
Nicolaus Anziani.
Adjutor in Bibl. Mediceo—L."

The question is one of much interest with theologians, and it will be seen by the above extract in the Assistant Librarian's letter, that the Florentine Copy of the Decree, by improperly using the word *etiam* instead of *et* in the Latin version as the equivalent for the first καὶ in the Greek, supports that reading which makes for the Pope's absolute supremacy over the whole Church.

This Council was an ineffectual attempt at a reconciliation and union between the churches of East and West, for although after long debates and delays the Decree for establishing such union was ultimately signed by the Representatives of both Churches, yet it was afterwards rejected by the whole body of the Orthodox Easterns.

www.ingramcontent.com/pod-product-compliance
Lightning Source LLC
Chambersburg PA
CBHW031600170426
43196CB00032B/648